INSPIRED TO ACTION

HOW FOLLOWING THE PROMPTINGS OF YOUR HEART CAN CHANGE THE WORLD

BY

REBECCA M. PRATT

CONTENTS

Some of the names have been changed to protect the identity of various individuals in Inspired to Action.

DEDICATION

This book is dedicated to all the hurting and suffering people in the world who need someone to fight for them.

I also dedicate this book to my precious dad, Bob Taylor, who modeled an adventurous and loving God to me through all of his life. He is an incredible storyteller who always brings everything back to Christ. He has been a great representative of God here on earth both to me and all those in his path.

ACKNOWLEDGMENTS

I want to thank God for allowing me to partner with Him in these incredible stories. This is His book. Not mine!

Thanks to Tim, my dear husband and best friend who enables me to live this dream. To my precious kids – Brianna, Desa'ree and Joshua – who inspire me to keep fighting for those who do not have the opportunities in life that they have been given.

Thanks to the many faithful family, friends, supporters, co-workers, pastors and advocates who each played a role in these inspirational stories. These are your stories too.

To all those who shaped this book through counsel and advice: David O'Connor, you were priceless in the last editorial process as you know; Shannon Ethridge, who mentored me in this writing project, I am so grateful for you. Patrick Butler, David Chapman, Andrew Tyler, Elena Pellizzaris, Amanda Potter and Bob Taylor Jr. who put time into the beginning editorial process. Each of you added invaluable advice. Book cover design by Emily Traynor — thank you for your beautiful work.

The Book Cover

The cover picture was inspired by a little girl at one of the orphanage homes where we work who was very sick. She had open, infected sores oozing all over her skin.

The hands you see extending towards the hurting girl belong to ladies who were living in the women's homeless shelter at the Lake Burien Presbyterian Church in Washington where we have our office. Each of them is now living on their own and working hard to get back on their feet. They have dreams to help others once they get the healing they need.

These women represent the people who have deep wounds from the world. Once given the opportunity to help themselves, they thrive and can in turn help others. They have a brokenness and humility that can only come from personally walking through tough times.

Another symbolic element are the large black hands that stand out bolder than the rest. To me, this symbolizes how in Africa it should be the Africans helping themselves and foreigners coming alongside them, enabling them to get started. God has given them the keys to change Africa.

COMMENTS ABOUT
INSPIRED TO ACTION

"This book was a riveting read. I felt like I was given insight into Rebecca's journey in a very personal manner. It is an inspiring and challenging experience. As we read her account, we face our own fears and find the courage to take action on behalf of those in need."

-Steve Martin, CEO, Love146

"This account of an exceptional undertaking in Africa is a challenge to anyone who struggles with the question of why so many of our world's children are allowed to suffer. It is a thought-provoking narrative that will help shape your outlook on these burning issues. Inspired to Action is an inspiration to abandon the ordinary and live a life fully committed to following God's promptings and leadings as we walk in accord with His will."

-David O'Connor, CFRE, Owner,
Five Oaks Consulting

"Rebecca Pratt is one of my heroes, and a hero to thousands of children. She isn't afraid of anyone who tries to stand in her way, even if that person is twice her tiny size! She is a modern-day David, slaying the giants of extreme poverty and injustice, and she'll inspire you to make a difference in this world as well."

-Shannon Ethridge, M.A., Best-selling Author,
Speaker & Certified Life Coach

"Rebecca's words are very powerful and important. I have been to Africa and have studied foreign aid in graduate school and deeply appreciate Rebecca's holistic, relationship – based approach to helping others. Her words have challenged me to follow some of my dreams for my community. Thank you Rebecca!"

-Amanda Potter, MSW

"After reading Rebecca's amazing story, I feel deeply moved. It makes me genuinely wonder what more I could be doing with my gifts, talents and blessings to the glory of God. This is a call to action for me and I thank God for Rebecca. Now I need to do something."

-Ben Malor, Chief Executive Producer,
United Nations Radio, New York

Introduction to Inspired to Action

God is daily giving us opportunities to work in partnership with Him. He is prompting our hearts to do something, anything – sometimes small, sometimes great.

The question is: are we listening? And if we hear, are we willing to step out of our comfort zones and be inconvenienced for the sake of seeing a miracle come to pass? Every day there are adventures waiting around the corner when we choose to partner with God.

Two years ago I was celebrating my 40th birthday in Newport Beach, California with my aunts and female cousins when the challenge came for me to put these stories into writing. I do not journal often, but I do love to tell real-life stories, especially stories of the amazing things that God has done.

All weekend, these ladies picked my brain for story after story of Africa, orphans and just plain old life. When the weekend was over and we were packing to leave, two of them asked if I had any of these stories in writing. I told them that I really did not have any time to do that, due to my full schedule. One of my aunts urged me to at least put the stories on tape so I would have a documentation of the things God has accomplished through my life. I brushed it off with, "Maybe in another life I will have time for something like that, but not in the near future." Then I was off to the airport.

I had a very restless sleep the first night after I arrived home in Texas. God started to genuinely convict my heart that these were His stories and they needed to be written down. God reminded me that in the Old Testament of the Bible when He did a radical miracle, He would tell His people to make a monument or record the story. This was to ensure they would never forget His faithfulness or His miracles. The people were to record them and always share them with others as a reminder of God's faithfulness. In the same way, I knew God was asking me to begin documenting the big things He had done in and through my life, too. I was never to forget.

That very night, in my sleeplessness, I started typing out the first stories. While writing, I had no idea of the impact these experiences would have on me as I relived them on my computer. While I wrote, many times I had tears streaming down my face.

I also had no idea that this experience would cause me to fall even more in love with God as I took a second look at all the details of what He has done in the lives of so many. The miracles I have witnessed are unbelievable. It is my prayer that you also fall more in love with God as you experience these stories. These are His stories that came about through His great love for all mankind.

Over the past 13 years, my husband Tim and I have traveled the world in a variety of capacities. For eight years we worked with an international medical mission called Mercy Ships. For six of those years we were in Texas running young adult training programs, and the rest of the time we were in Africa aboard one of their hospital ships. Since the completion of our time with Mercy Ships, we have been working full-time as co-founders of Orphan Relief and Rescue. We now reside in Seattle.

My life's passion is to inspire people to action on behalf of people who are suffering domestically and internationally. I have come to the conclusion that a life unto myself is no life at all. My hope is that through this book you will come to understand what your role is in God's larger story.

Everyone wants to leave a mark on this earth, to make a difference somehow, somewhere. That is how God created us to exist. Our fulfillment in life is directly connected to our relationship with God and our service to others. We were meant to live this life in partnership with Him.

Each of us have our own stories of hardships and difficulties that have brought us to a level of brokenness we have had to walk through. Many of us have become battered and worn out. Some of us become bitter because of what we have had to endure. Others choose to run to God and allow hardships to bring us to a new level of humility and sensitivity towards others who are going through tough things themselves. If we have chosen to go down the latter road, then the healing process has awakened us to a whole new level of compassion, allowing us to extend a healing hand to those who we may not have been able to reach before we experienced deep pain. This, my friend, becomes the precious touch of God flowing from our lives.

My hope and prayer is that you will be awakened to what you were made to be and what you were meant to do in this world – to live fully alive. May you get a glimpse of what it will take for you to leave the dark cellar of a battered life and experience the life which is destined for you.

We only get one shot at life. Let's not waste our days living for ourselves. Let's live to the fullest as God intended until we take our last breath.

Sometimes living to the fullest occurs when we allow ourselves to experience the pain that others suffer. The stories in this book are not easy reading or subject matter, but they are very important. Some of the stories I write are hard to fully take in. They deal with human trafficking, hurting children and other dark and painful, yet very real situations. I tell them not to depress you, but rather to educate and show what God is doing in some of the harshest places in the world.

-Rebecca Pratt, September 2011

~~~~~~~~~

CHAPTER 1

BROKEN HEART

~~~~~~~~~

"Whenever you find tears in your eyes, especially unexpected tears, it is well to pay the closet attention. They are not only telling the secret of who you are, but more often than not of the mystery of where you have come from and are summoning you to where you should go next."

–Frederick Buechner, "Whistling in the Dark"

One frightful day in 2010, a terrified young African girl was bound and gagged as she was abducted off the streets of Benin on her way to school. Scared and confused about why this man had forcefully taken her to his village, she cried and shook violently. The sheer terror of the next few hours after her abduction can hardly be fathomed. She was placed on a makeshift altar prepared for the Voodoo ritual that would lead this man to murder her in cold blood. Nine other young girls would endure the same trauma over his three–month killing spree. This killer was required to sacrifice ten virgin girls to appease his god, so one by one, each young girl was viciously murdered.

Sacrificing humans has been outlawed for years in this nation, yet stories like this are not uncommon in Benin, which is known as the Voodoo capital of the world. In this instance the man was caught and put into prison. But some are not. In many villages, a child – particularly an orphan – does not carry any worth as a sacred human life.

Now rewind the calendar to February 2005, to my first discovery of this value system.

My husband Tim and I and our three kids were working full-time on a hospital ship called the Anastasis operated by Mercy Ships International. Tim and I were responsible for a field team working upcountry, three hours from the ship. The team had communicated with us in vivid detail about the awful plight of the orphan children they had met. They desperately wanted some answers about how they could help these children out of their terrible situation as they were met with one disappointment after another. Realizing that unless we saw the situation with our own eyes, we could not really give adequate advice, we decided to take the three-hour journey upcountry to check things out.

Nothing could have prepared Tim and me for what we experienced when we drove up to a little mud-block orphanage housing 109 hungry and sick children in rural Benin. As barefoot and roughly-dressed children came up to greet us by the dozen, I could not help but look deeply into their hollow eyes and see that they were in serious trouble. The children swarmed our healthy, strange bodies and began to grab our hands. There was deep interest in our unusual white skin. I reached down and picked up a little girl who seemed desperately eager to be held. As I cuddled her in my arms, I realized she had skin lice, fungal growths and open, infected wounds taking over her little body. She scratched herself constantly, clearly miserable in her own skin.

My heart instantly began to break for her and for all the other kids living in that home. The orphanage director told me the children were between the ages of two and sixteen. All 109 of them lived in a four-room structure with no water, toilets or showers. Each one ate about half a cup of rice a day and it showed in their tiny limbs. Many, including the smallest ones, had visible hernias from carrying five-gallon water jugs almost three miles many times each day, walking barefoot over rocky terrain.

I looked more closely at all the children's bodies, as my motherly tendencies were taking over. I had never seen such disease and neglect. Some of the children wore nothing more than underwear, highlighting their bony ribs, skinny arms and legs, and distended bellies.

The director, Mr. Kouto, greeted us and guided us on a tour of the home. Inside the children's living spaces there were no beds or furniture, no place to put clothes – only worn-out bags with a few odd pieces of clothing sitting in the corners of each of the three bedrooms. The floors were just hard-packed dirt, and I was shown how the kids would put down grass mats to sleep on at night. A desk and a few wooden chairs constituted an office. None of the rooms had windows. The darkness inside this so-called home reflected the deep despair that grew in my heart with each step I took.

Finally we broke out of the darkness into welcome daylight. Walking around the back of the home, I noticed miniature stick crosses stuck awkwardly into the ground. When I asked Mr. Kouto about it, he casually said it was the kids' play area. I thought it was interesting that the kids were carving crosses out of sticks but didn't press further on that first visit. Months later, I was told that this play area was where the orphans were buried when they died, the rudely carved crosses the only markers for their tiny graves.

Even more disturbing was what the Mayor's office later informed me – no death certificate was required for an orphan in that part of the country. When an orphan died, they could legally be buried in the back yard. No questions asked by anyone, no paperwork of any kind provided.

The survivors' memories would be the only record of that particular precious child's existence.

I began to question Mr. Kouto. "Why would you take in kids if you cannot afford to care for them or feed them?" I became very direct, asking him many penetrating questions, trying to understand how such a ghastly situation could exist.

He described the overwhelming number of orphans in his area that ended up on the streets because few were willing to help them. He said the social welfare office has no other place near him even accepting children. The orphanages on the outskirts of town were all full. Many times, relatives took orphans only to use them as domestic servants. I eventually learned this is a common practice throughout Benin.

In the city of Cotonou alone, a study done in 2007 by the US State Department reported there were over 250,000 children in domestic servitude. Some were orphans and others were from families in difficult circumstances that sent their children to earn their keep in someone else's home. [1]

He added that when the social welfare office approaches him with a child, his hand is forced because the child has nowhere else to go. That's when children are most vulnerable, he said, and they end up living on the street. "They are then used for terrible purposes," he told me.

Most kids caught in that situation die or are trafficked into the sex and labor trades.[2] "I would rather they die with me, having known love, than die with no love."

Reeling from this sordid scenario, I could not fathom having to make such decisions. I was at a complete loss for words. I asked him what the hardest thing was that he had to deal with in this line of work. He didn't even pause, immediately replying it was when the little ones cried themselves to sleep at night due to hunger. He said it was a terrible thing to hear – and even worse – not being able to bring them relief.

Another difficult thing, he told me, was when the children were really sick and he had no money to take them to the hospital. The children had to watch their friends go through immense pain when they were sick, many giving up and dying in their midst. This was very traumatic for all of them, young and old. The sheer reality of this conversation completely floored me as a mom.

My friends sometimes tell me I have a business mindset; I am a problem solver who finds it easy to crunch numbers, gather resources, motivate others to action and see a solution brought to concrete reality. As he spoke, my business mind began spinning, and I started pouring out questions. I wanted to know how he got any money, and how they were even able to pay rent and buy food each month.

Mr. Kouto was a schoolteacher making only sixty dollars a month. Fifty dollars went to rent and the remaining ten dollars was all that remained for food. He said it was all he could do. He was doing his best the only way he knew.

Mr. Kouto was proud of his accomplishments as a director. He made sure that all the children attended school and were well educated. He believed education was the most important thing for the kids. He was very strict in this regard because he was a teacher and knew how important a good education was for their future. Each night by candlelight the children did all their homework. As he was speaking, I was looking at one of the older boys leaning over his homework at the only desk in the home. He looked lethargic and tired and seemed to lack the motivation to study. There was little life in the eyes of many of the children due to the malnutrition, disease and death all around them.

My thoughts silently fought against his reasoning: the children were dying! Many would not even make it to their eighteenth birthday. Education is useless without food and medicine and sanitary conditions. They can study all they want, but if their bodies are wasting away, their brains are certainly not going to retain anything. Our whole conversation seemed crazy.

As I was trying to make sense of it all, it soon became evident that this was probably the only way Mr. Kouto knew how to handle an impossible situation – planning in hope for the children's future was his coping mechanism. He was a teacher; it was all he knew to do. He had to focus the kids on something, right? Taking their minds off of being hungry and sick, I am sure, was his constant challenge. Mr. Kouto was doing his best to give the children hope for a future, even in the face of the grim reality that many would not live long. My mind was buckling under the implications.

I asked him how hard he had tried to get food and help for these kids within the local community, because I knew there were many foreign aid and human rights organizations around. He explained how he had gone to many of them for help, with no success, and was at a loss for what else he could do. Some neighbors dropped off food occasionally, but this only helped on a small scale.

Tim and I began spending more time with the children. A little boy who was about three years old, Fabrice, caught our attention. He had a severely distended stomach ballooning from malnutrition. He wore a tattered gold African outfit and walked with a little waddle, always resting his hands behind his back. He carried himself like a king, yet always very slowly, and he looked at the ground as he went.

When Tim picked Fabrice up, the child nuzzled right into his chest and immediately dozed off, safe and secure. Fabrice had a hard time approaching any females in our group because his mother had beaten him so severely that he had almost died. The neighbors saved him and brought him to the orphanage – a mixed blessing.

Tim melted while this little guy was in his arms. I knew immediately he was forming a real bond with sweet Fabrice. When it was time to leave, Tim had a very difficult time putting him down, knowing the hopeless environment we were leaving Fabrice to live in. Although he was no longer beaten by his mother and was loved, there was no future for him. Once our team left, his little belly would be empty once again within a few weeks.

The memory of Fabrice's face and body would haunt us both. We knew he had no future without outside intervention. A high percentage of children in these awful conditions would never see their fifth birthday.[3] As a mother, my heart was bleeding. I was crushed inside as I held each little one.

Rural Benin was truly the most needy, heart-wrenching place I had ever seen up to that point in my travels. I did not know how to handle any of the emotions I was experiencing. I was in complete and utter despair. I could not discern any viable answer for these children. The problem in front of me was simply too big, too complex – yet the eyes of Fabrice and all the other little ones continued to haunt me to the core of my being.

While processing the field team's disappointments more thoroughly, we found out the local pastor assigned to this team was corrupt in every area of his life; he had made it quite obvious that personal gain was his top priority and that he would not be of any help to us. Our team had also spoken with different organizations who had local field offices about providing assistance to the orphanage home but to no avail. Our own field budget was also very limited.

Through the assessment process we learned that the home was rented, which meant that any structural upgrades we might be able to make could actually cause the landlord to raise the rent. The only thing our team could do in the short term was start providing a couple of meals each day and drive the children to fill up their water jugs in our vehicle. It didn't seem like much, but we thought it would stop some immediate suffering.

Saving the little ones from walking those strenuous miles each day to fetch water turned out to be a huge improvement. Seeing young children lug heavy jugs, each one weighing around 45 pounds, such a long distance was a sight to see. There were no wheelbarrows, just little bodies dragging these jugs for miles, inch by inch, foot by foot, until they reached home. Within an hour or so, they would have to turn around and do it all over again. It was absolutely crazy to witness. It was such a hopeless situation with no easy answers.

After returning to the *Anastasis* in the port of Cotonou, our hearts were completely broken.

It was at this time that my entire perception of the world hit the fan. I realized what I thought was reality was not reality at all. It was my own illusion, which gave me no sense of responsibility for things happening in the world beyond what was directly in front of me.

My world had been very narrow for so long, like a grain of sand. My tiny perspective was all I knew, and I didn't even know how to begin processing this new reality.

It was a time for introspection; would I be able to live fully awakened to what was really going on around me in the world, this world of so much injustice? Was I ready to allow myself to hurt deeply alongside those in so much pain?

When Tim and I arrived back at the ship that evening, our three children, who at the time were fifteen, twelve and ten, were all lying peacefully in their comfortable beds. Looking at their healthy bodies was a stark contrast compared to the orphans we had seen that day. Our kids never went to bed hungry. They never went without medicine. Our children did not lack anything they needed; yet those children lacked everything. They had plenty of clean clothes and numerous pairs of shoes in their closets. How could life be so unfair? Who was going to fight for the lives and futures of these orphaned children?

In my turmoil, I took the next day to be alone and process everything we had just experienced. I prayed that God would save the helpless children we had met that day and intervene with a miracle in their lives.

As I read my Bible, all I saw were verses about not turning our backs on the orphans and widows, and about God's incredible love for them. I prayed for God to bring wealthy people through to see the kids, so that they could help them. I knew that we were barely keeping up with our bills, so we could not personally take on such an enormous financial challenge.

I wanted to yell far and wide to whoever would listen, "Please help these children!" I pleaded with God through these Scriptures for the lives of Fabrice and the many other children in the home.

> *"Open your ears, God, to my prayer; don't pretend you*
> *don't hear me knocking.*
> *Come close and whisper your answer.*
> *I really need you."*
>
> *(Ps 55:1a, The Message)*

I began to speak this prayer over the orphans' lives, anticipating that God was going to save them based on this passage in Psalms:

> *"God, you did everything you promised,*
> *and I'm thanking you with all my heart.*
> *You pulled them from the brink of death,*
> *their feet from the cliff-edge of doom.*

*Now they stroll at leisure with God
in the sunlit fields of life."*

(Ps 56:12-13, The Message)

I knew that I had to act on what God had allowed us to be exposed to. Calling different organizations in the area to see what the options were seemed like the logical place to start. Surely someone would come forward if they only knew how dire the circumstances were, I thought. But each phone call got the same response: "Oh, that's too bad. I am so sorry, but we cannot help orphanages in those conditions. These places become too dependent on us. If you help them, you had better be prepared to help them for life. This is not within the scope of what we can do within our organization."

I could not believe it. Organizations whose sole purpose was to help the dying were turning them away. I reeled with dismay.

My sleepless nights started when I felt like God was asking me to do something bigger than I felt I was able to do. I was about to get more than I bargained for. I fought back, knowing that a decision to act would cost me dearly – more than I was willing to give up. I made every excuse why I couldn't be involved: my responsibilities were as a wife and mother, and I had responsibilities on the hospital ship we were already serving. The more I processed it, the more I didn't think it was possible for me to actually do anything. And perhaps the most compelling reason of all: the ship was about to set sail, separating my family and me from the problem, maybe forever.

God had a plan and a purpose for those precious kids, but they had no future without someone helping them. Somebody had to say 'yes' in order for God to do what He wanted to do. I was just hoping it did not have to be me.

After three days and three long, sleepless nights, I was up at five a.m. with a full-fledged plan for how it could all work if God really wanted me to go help the kids in that little mud-block orphanage in rural Benin.

I wrote out a budget for a plan of action to rescue the children from their unimaginable circumstances. This two-year plan came to around $16,000. The immediate goal was to provide the means to keep them alive for the next two years and, in that time, come up with a long-term solution. This would include:

- A new rental home that would have sanitary conditions, water, toilets and showers
- Food to be dropped off monthly
- Doctor visits monthly
- Utilities, electricity and water

People would need to be recruited in Benin to continue implementing these things after my initial setup. Starting to e-mail friends about the need was also part of the plan; then we would wait and see what God would do to bring in the finances to make this a reality.

We were to set sail in just two weeks and my internal arguments continued. If I did not at least try to do something to help I would always wonder if I could have really made a difference in these kids' lives. What would be the loss in trying to help them, even if it ended in failure? They would be no worse off than they were now. So what would it really cost me personally? My time? My comfort? My pride? My name? Others' opinions of me? These were all selfish reasons not to do it. Yet, I thought, if I do try and this is a successful rescue mission, then these children will have a chance for a healthy life and future. There is no price tag we could ever put on this. I decided that the risk of trying was worthwhile; the consequences of doing nothing were unacceptable.

Because of my commitments to my family and my responsibilities on the ship, these four things needed to happen if I was to go forward: first, my boss on the ship would have to let me go upcountry for a week. Tim would have to let me go as well. A young friend of ours, a local doctor, would have to join me as a translator. And finally, the field team leaders would have to let my friend and me stay with them.

In one afternoon, all of these things were granted. My husband Tim was extremely supportive, because his heart was equally broken for the children. Without his full support, I could not have thought of going. My work leader granted me the time off for the initiative, my doctor/translator friend was eager to go and our field team leaders were very supportive of the idea.

As it sank in that I was going to move forward with this plan, I had to emotionally prepare myself for what I was getting into. The particular part of Benin where we would be focusing is a very dark place spiritually. The locals claim it is the birthplace of Voodoo. There are temples throughout almost every village, and the practice of Voodoo wraps magic and sorcery around every aspect of life. People claim that they use it to commune with the dead, as well as manipulate the living through curses and potions. Certain gods associated with this practice are appeased through blood sacrifices. Most often this is done using animals in the Voodoo temples, but we soon learned about the reality of human sacrifice in these pagan rituals.

As we walked down the street where the orphanage was located upcountry, it was not uncommon to have people chant curses at us. At their city's edge there was a huge statue of a king with his arm outstretched. A sign below it read "White Man No Pass. Say No To Colonization." This was a symbol of the past when the French came in with the intention of changing the Africans' way of life. Entering this area of the city could be a bit daunting for a newcomer who was white.

I was not naïve enough to think our plan to reach out to the children would be easy. My personal preference would have been not to take on such a large endeavor in a place like this. There were just too many things that could go wrong. Yet here I was preparing to go while knowing in my heart that it was exactly what I was supposed to do.

CHAPTER 2

SAYING YES

*"Faith does not operate in the realm of the possible.
There is no glory for God in that which is humanly
possible. Faith begins where man's power ends."*

– George Mueller

*"And surely I am with you always, to the very end
of the age"*

– Matthew 28:20 (NIV)

At the age of nine, Amina became an orphan in Benin after a motorbike accident killed her parents. An uncle took her into his home and used her as a domestic servant in his household of six. No special privileges were provided for her as a relative. In his mind it was the will of the gods that destined her to become an orphan. Therefore he was justified to treat her as the lowest rung of society. It would now be her duty to be in service to others for the duration of her childhood.

She endured verbal abuse and numerous random beatings from her uncle. Amina later told us she worked from sun-up until far into the night, never able to take a real rest. Her brother and sister were also placed in relatives' homes and endured the same treatment. There was no time for mourning her dead parents. Amina admitted that she was numb for years after their death, totally unable to grieve the loss of her entire family. She often filled her pillow with tears in the darkness of the night when no one could see her.

When she turned 14 years old, her uncle saw the opportunity to make a profit from his niece. He bargained with a Muslim man for a large sum of money and sold her to become one of his many wives. A whole new type of torture, she said, began with the man who called himself her husband. She was raped regularly and brutally beaten daily. Each day Amina felt she would not live through the horrific torture. She knew if she did not escape, her life would end at a young age. Almost a year passed before she was able to run away. When the man was out of town, she escaped to another village. She begged for food on the streets of Benin until she was rescued by a social worker who noticed this newcomer in town.

The social welfare offices had been alerted of the human trafficking going on within their town and were advised to keep their eyes open for wandering street children. Amina was easy prey for the professional traffickers looking for innocent, unsuspecting girls in her exact situation who were living on the streets to escape their abusive lives. Amina had no idea how lucky she was when a caring social worker took notice of her. She was taken to the only orphanage home still accepting children. All the others were full. This home already had too many mouths to feed, but they took her in anyway.

Amina had been in the home just a few months when we met her. She was frail and weak but thankful not to be enduring an abusive situation any longer.

Due to excruciating poverty in many parts of Africa, even very young girls are trapped in similar circumstances and sold into marriage. Others are trafficked in the sex or

domestic service trades at the hands of heartless oppor-
tunists attempting to make money from a child's misery.
A UNICEF study done in 2006 recorded 40,000 children
trafficked to, from or through Benin.[4] In a small country
of only eight million people, these numbers are staggering.

The U.S State Department published a report in
2009 revealing more than half of Benin's internally trafficked children are taken to Cotonou – the country's
main port city. From there, a high percentage of them
are taken out of the country for a life of servitude or
slavery. Within the country, girls are trafficked primarily
for domestic servitude and sexual exploitation. Boys are
subjected to forced agricultural and construction work,
street hawking and handicraft activities. Those who are
taken from Benin to other African countries are sold for
the same purposes, plus forced labor in mines and stone
quarries.

This report also stated that the Government of Benin
did not fully comply with even minimum standards for the
elimination of trafficking. The report did acknowledge they
were making significant efforts to do so, despite limited
resources. During the time of the study, Benin was enact-
ing strong anti-trafficking victim protection and prevention
measures, making strident efforts toward complying with
international standards. [5]

When the report was made public, tremendous pressure
was put on the Beninese government to enforce the anti-
trafficking laws put in place by the U.S. State Department
and other agencies within the country. Progress is slow, but
each year we are seeing more traffickers caught and incar-
cerated, and more children rescued. In the last two years
we have also seen increased safeguards put into place to
protect children. Despite what seems to be an uphill battle
much of the time, we are encouraged with the progress that
has been achieved.

A significant new awareness has been brought to this issue, and many locals are being challenged to change their way of thinking towards children and orphans. Today the social welfare offices and government officials are on high alert – many have become my personal heroes as they have taken up the fight against abuse and human trafficking in their towns.

As we began moving forward with our plan to relocate the 109 kids in our target village to a safer environment, we had no idea this orphanage home was right in the center of one of the largest child trafficking routes in all of Africa. We would later find out the home was actually being used as a safe house for many of the children, protecting them from the horrors of life as a child slave or worse as in the case of Amina.

For the next 10 days, our friend Dr. Carel became my voice in this French-speaking nation. As both an educated black national and a doctor, he was the perfect person to help me with negotiations. There could not have been a better translator, cultural advisor and negotiator for the job. I was equally excited that Dr. Carel would be able to assess and treat sick children at the orphanage. He had recently finished his studies in medicine at the University in Cotonou and had been practicing a short time in a local hospital when we met him. We became instant friends after he showed up to help the ship's mission when we arrived in Benin. Dr. Carel immediately had our attention due to his very welcoming smile and his kind mannerisms.

Now we had a new mission to accomplish together. Standing in a crowded parking lot full of taxicabs in the city of Cotonou, he negotiated with a driver to get us upcountry, a three-hour journey. The reality of what we were setting out to do started to sink in. I could not believe I was going forward with this huge plan to relocate 109 kids. It suddenly seemed absolutely crazy. This was my first real

African adventure without my 6-foot-5-inch husband at my side. Tim had always made me feel completely safe no matter what scenario we were in. Now I was on my own with Dr. Carel, prepared to see what God was going to do with all of this.

We were scheduled to depart from Benin on the *Anastasis* in just two weeks. We had been living and working on the ship for about six months at that point. The *Anastasis* was a 159-meter hospital ship with approximately 350 people from 30 different nations living on board. Having originally been launched over 50 years ago, it had seen better days, but it was functional for its purpose in Africa. Thousands of people have acquired free surgeries on board this vessel over its 29 years of service to the poorest of the poor.

I knew timing alone would have to be nothing short of miraculous to accomplish anything significant. All my major internal battles had already been fought while I was sitting safe and secure on the ship. The words that I felt God echo in my mind were, "Just give me your hands, feet, and mouth, and I will do the rest." I knew this was not going to be comfortable. I just had to keep my focus on God and the task set before me.

While driving, I loved soaking in all the African scenery. There were banana trees surrounding the numerous mud huts. Naked little children played close to their topless mamas. Young boys holding up freshly killed snakes stood by the roadside to sell them to passing vehicles. Women carried timber three times their weight on their heads with babies on their backs. This was storybook Africa.

On the other hand, there were scenes not so pleasant to look at, such as all of the coffin-making businesses on the sides of the road. They came in various shapes and sizes. Some were smaller ones meant for babies and children. This was the dose of reality that brought my thoughts back to why we were even on this journey. The mortality rate in

Benin is extremely high. Only one in six children will make it to their fifth birthday. [6]

Upon arrival upcountry, we found the field team extremely discouraged and even depressed. After only five weeks in this very spiritually dark place, most of them were ready to go home and call it quits. They had encountered incredible roadblocks while trying to help the people. They felt in their final few weeks of service that they had run out of time to really accomplish anything of significance. The team was spiritually and physically beaten down. Even after around-the-clock prayer times, they had not seen any tangible results among the people they had come to serve.

While they were depressed emotionally, they did not realize the spiritual impact they were actually making in the unseen world in preparation for what God wanted to accomplish. They had been setting the spiritual ground-work without even realizing it.

Not long after the team moved into their rented home, a Muslim neighbor knocked on their door to ask them how long they were going to stay. Not understanding his motive, a team member began inquiring about his line of questions. The neighbor explained that from the time their team had come to live next door, the bad spirits had not tormented his family. He said each night they were tormented, but for some reason they had not been since the team arrived. He wanted to know how much longer his family could antici-pate good night's sleep.

This was a great testimony to the team of the power we carry within us when we are walking close with God. Not to mention the opportunity this team had to share about the one and only true and all-powerful God. **We have no idea how our everyday lives affect the unseen spirit world around us, wherever we go and whatever we do.**

As we all gathered that first evening, I laid out my plan with great excitement. To my dismay, these ambitious ideas were not received with much enthusiasm. The questions the team asked were filled with doubt. For a group so emotionally involved with these kids, I was sure this news would bring hope to them. On the other hand, I did not understand the emotionally despairing place the team was really in. After that evening talk I had to fight my own discouragement. What made me think I would see different results than them in that town? Who did I think I was anyway?

That evening I could clearly hear the Voodoo drums playing in the distance. I realized I had to stay very focused to keep myself from falling into deep discouragement. Hour by hour I had to be conscious of giving all my emotions to God. This was all His! God was either going to make this plan happen, or it was all going to be one big flop. I completely released it to Him numerous times a day.

The team leaders, Sam Garner and Robin Trostad, were great in trying to encourage the team to stay strong and encouraged. This was not easy. They were young leaders around the age of 25 with a tough assignment. I have a lot of respect for them in how they handled many of the difficulties that came their way.

While the unseen was happening in the spiritual realm, there were also visible things occurring that were not fun. At 6 a.m. each morning a naked man would bang on the door outside our concrete fence. When one of the team members answered the door, the man would run away, leaving a dead rat at the top of our fence. The dead rodent symbolized a certain curse he was placing on us. This is a common practice in Benin when someone wants you to go away. This was a constant reminder we were not welcomed by some of the neighbors. This was only one of many incidents that would happen while we were there.

Nothing was comfortable by any means. Sleeping was extremely difficult as mice would scurry over our bodies in the night. A constant companion, sweat and dirt seemed to stick to every inch of my body throughout the day. A lack of running water made bucketing from the well a necessity in order to function. Nightly noises like Voodoo drums and random screaming could be heard throughout the neighborhood. Staying focused was a real challenge with the many distractions of simply surviving.

On the first morning there Robin and I went straight to the Mayor's office with Dr. Carel to find out all we could about the orphanage and its director. They informed us the director was a good man who didn't turn away kids in need. We questioned the Mayor about why he would allow children to live in such conditions, and his response was that many children in two-parent households in the area lived in similar types of conditions. "This is just due to poverty," he said. "Just look around. Please do not leave without helping us."

That afternoon in the Mayor's office we laid out our two-year plan along with the Mayor's Project Director. We shared that we had no money at the present, but we were going to trust that God would help us raise enough money to relocate the orphanage to adequate housing and take care of utilities and monthly food deliveries. After two years, I would return to help make plans for the kids' future.

The Project Director was totally confused by our comment that we did not have any money at that time and voiced his deep concern. We were then able to explain the God element in the situation. Only God could really make this all work, and we were choosing to believe that God was going to do His will, even though we had no money in hand yet. We told him we were not making any promises. We were just going to walk forward and watch God work. We told him God loved and valued those kids more than any of us, and if God wanted this to happen, it would happen.

He pleaded with us not to have expectations that anything would happen as quickly as we needed. He committed to helping us however he could, but he did not want us to get discouraged. He said, "This is Africa, and nothing ever happens quickly here." We told him, "Our team has two more weeks, so let's see what happens." We shook hands, and off we went excited to move forward with the blessing of the "Chief of the Village" (the Mayor and area Project Director). We have learned over the years that this is always the first step in healthy Community Development endeavors.

The next thing on the list was to talk to the orphanage director, Mr. Kouto, to make sure he was in agreement with the plan. When we arrived at the home, Mr. Kouto was not there, but the younger children who were not in school came running out to greet us. Their dirty, infected skin and frail, thin bodies again pierced my heart.

Dr. Carel took a close look at them and pointed out the urgency of getting them medical help. The children were in serious trouble and Dr. Carel was extremely disturbed by what he saw. He showed me in detail what each child suffered from as he inspected their bodies. Open wounds had turned to dangerous staph infections. Lice covered their scalps and bodies. A deep black fungus marred some of their frail bodies – it would be dangerous if left untreated. He also drew my attention to the bony little bodies and bloated stomachs caused by severe malnourishment. It was not easy looking closer at the reality of it all, particularly through the eyes of a medical professional.

As we were walking away from the orphanage home, the urgency for Fabrice and the other kids to be rescued swept over me. All the small children began to follow us up the long dirt road. I kept looking behind me to shoo them back, for fear they would follow us too far away from their home. They were only dressed in little panties, and their large distended stomachs and bony little arms sparked some very familiar scenes from those "Feed the Hungry" commercials that I saw as a child on television. I recalled making a mental commitment to someday help the hungry little children around the world. Tears flooded my eyes as this childhood dream was now standing before me in a very desperate and real way.

The realization of "my dream" caught me completely off guard. I was reeling from this personal revelation. While I was lost in the moment, God graciously spoke to my heart, "You think this is your dream, but in reality this is "My dream" which I have placed in you. These are my babies whom I love more than you could ever imagine." I was suddenly struck by God's plan to give us dreams that are from His heart. These dreams really aren't our own; they are His, which we get to share in with Him. Wow! The emotions of that moment were absolutely overwhelming. "Oh God," I said, "You are going to help us rescue these kids." **There was no doubt in my mind after that moment, this whole plan was going to happen because these were His babies and this was His dream to rescue them from starvation, abuse, despair, neglect and early death**!

When we were finally able to meet up with Mr. Kouto and two Peace Corp volunteers working in the area, they showed great excitement about the plan. So we continued to walk forward.

Connecting with other organizations in the area was next on the list. These organizations were afraid of creating dependency on their services. However, eventually a few individuals within the organizations were persuaded to help on a personal level with certain logistics, which was critical in the implementation of the plan. The Peace Corps volunteers were also a vital part.

The Mayor's office put out a plea on the radio for anyone with a large home for rent to call in. We recruited many in the community to help us find a place for the kids, which ended up being an exhausting process culturally.

This is when I found out that every successful business deal in Africa is done through relationship. It was not about the business at hand, it was all about building friendships. Once a friendship was established, then they would determine if they wanted to rent their home to me or not. Getting a home for these kids was dependent on hours and hours of relationship building. My Western business mind had to die completely in this whole process. Dr. Carel was critical in helping me understand how to walk through this culturally.

After ten days we found a home that had running water, electricity, a large backyard, toilets, showers and sinks. This was a perfect place for the children and was within walking distance of their school.

In sharing the need via email, $22,000 was raised in five days. People all over the world gave sacrificially.

When it was time to move the kids in, Tim came to help us. He had made so many personal sacrifices to enable me to do this, so it was fun to share this incredible celebration with him.

Singing, clapping and constant smiles filled the vehicle while we transported them to their new home. They could hardly contain their excitement. When we drove up to their house they started shaking and screaming like what you see on the TV show "Extreme Makeover". They zoomed out of the vehicle and ran all over the place, running room to room, checking every detail out. Toilets, light switches, sinks, walls, doors, fans, they had to touch everything to just make sure it was real. It was so much fun to watch. Such a great day! Little did they know that their chance of survival had just significantly increased simply from their change of environment.

The team members worked very hard getting everything ready for the kids to move in. On moving day they had to train them how to use a flushing toilet, wash their hands with running water and use a light switch for power. This was a very rewarding experience for the whole team. They were able to share in the huge blessing of watching God answer the hundreds of prayers that they had prayed for the kids with names like Rosalie, Espetite, Ghislain, Fabrice and the many others they had grown to love. This became the highlight of their field assignment.

Mercy Ship friends were also able to join the celebrations before we sailed out of the country, and some of them even built tables and benches to bless the kids.

Before leaving Benin, a two-year contract was signed for the home. The Mayor's signature was on every document, to make sure no one would try to bring corruption issues into the deal. The Project Director still shakes his head in amazement when we talk about how this rescue mission all came together. He said he has never seen anything like this happen in all of Benin in the time frame we experienced. "Things like this do not happen here," he said. I always remind him that God was the determining factor in this whole plan. God definitely proved His love for these precious ones!

Through years of being involved with the children in this town, we have built priceless relationships with the local Mayor's office and social welfare department. On my recent trip in 2010, the Project Director and Mayor wrote an amazing letter of recommendation for us. This is a small portion of their letter, hand-delivered to me in May of 2010. I have purposely left the town name out as to protect the reputation of the area in which we are working.

We have seen [Orphan Relief and Rescue's] commitment and professionalism in their engagement with the success of their projects. Rebecca Pratt has received the complete support in her pursuit of projects helping the children in this town. We hereby certify that Madame Rebecca Pratt and her NGO are reliable and recommend them to both National and International organizations for the development work around the world and particularly in our town.

They have since asked us to do more projects to help many more children in need.

As the details of setting up this new home for the kids went into motion, food was dropped off monthly, doctor services were set up for regular assistance and immunization given. The two Peace Corps volunteers trained the children and director on numerous life skills, as well as made sure things ran smoothly. A children's minister also donated his time on Saturdays to implement a program for the kids to learn more about God.

Our friend Dr. Carel was deeply affected by everything that he got to be a part of. He wrote many emails after we left about how God was speaking to him about his future through this experience. This is part of an email that he wrote:

The Lord spoke to me last night and told me that He has chosen me to take care of the orphan kids who have no future because of their miserable situations. I pray the Lord will fortify me, to make spiritual provision for me to reach this mission. The Holy Spirit revealed to me that I am an ambassador of the Kingdom of Heaven here on earth. The Lord has mandated this great mission on me and I asked God to give me wisdom in this. I am so humbled to be the Lord's tool in my country Benin. I will do my best for these children.

He soon started a rural clinic ministry for people in different villages in addition to working a full-time job. He is now in Canada furthering his medical education with aspirations of returning to his native country to serve his people through medicine. He tells me that he has not forgotten all that God has spoken to him.

Through this time I fell in love with the Beninese people. They truly captured my heart. They are an amazing and beautiful people who are passionate, hard-working, creative and refined in many ways. They dress to the hilt in bright cultural African attire even if they live in mud huts.

Looking nice is very important to them. They express polite curiosity toward those who have come to their country, and are extra friendly when they realize you do not want to take anything from them. You have made a friend for life if they see there is not a selfish agenda on your part.

The leadership of Mercy Ships also played a huge part in allowing the team and me to take on such a project. This was outside of the scope of what they normally do, so I will forever be grateful to those who authorized us to go forward with the orphanage projects, as well as partners and donors who continue to be involved today.

It was a very humbling experience to be part of such a miraculous story. It was also exhilarating. We were all on a 'natural high' which was hard to explain due to the favor God gave us and the doors He opened. It was a huge adrenaline rush seeing all this accomplished. I felt like screaming on a mountaintop a huge "yes" to justice being served for all those children. This was God's plan all along; He just needed willing people who would implement it on His behalf.

This awakened something in me I never knew was there before. God got my attention. He wanted me to understand in a very tangible way that this is exactly how He intends the body of Christ to function. This is how nations will be transformed as we all rise up. This is how God created us to come alive and affect positive change in front of us. When He prompts our hearts to act and we walk forward, we carry God's power and strength within us. Once we accept Christ in our lives, we are given EVERYTHING to live this kind of life in partnership with Him. It is the life the apostle Paul was talking about in the book of Ephesians.

Spending ourselves on behalf of the less fortunate in this world is exactly what we were born to do. In our years as a family we had already been doing that on a smaller scale, but my faith in God had never been tested to this degree before my experience in Benin. My heart had never been so broken by what was in front of me. Watching God literally part the Red Sea as He did for those children built up my faith in a whole new way.

I came across a devotional by Oswald Chambers that described this so perfectly.

"If Jesus ever gave us a command He could not enable us to fulfill, He would be a liar, and if we make our inability a barrier to obedience, it means we are telling God there is something He has not taken into account. Every element of self-reliance must be slain by the power of God. Complete weakness and dependence will always be the occasion for the Spirit of God to manifest His power."

In my complete weakness, God showed me He was enough, just as it says in 2 Corinthians 12:9 *"My grace is sufficient for you, for power is perfected in weakness."*

Sailing north up the west coast of Africa towards Liberia, I watched the country of Benin fade into the distance with a full and grateful heart, knowing God accomplished everything He wanted to for 109 children. He rescued them from impending and premature death. He was giving them a quality of life that they could never have dreamed of if we had not followed His leading in obedience. Now it was time to prepare my heart for the next venture in Liberia. I had no idea what to expect. All I knew was we were going to arrive in a country that had just gone through a very bloody civil war and their people and nation were in shambles. With just over a year since the peace accord of 2003, it was estimated that 83% of the population was unemployed and most of the people were walking around with post-traumatic stress syndrome from witnessing brutality and death all around them. Most lost family members, or were witnesses to their torture or rape. The needs were endless and extreme. In just three short days I would be walking into a whole new reality that would be shockingly crippling for me.

Questions for Personal Reflection:

- What breaks your heart?

- Is God prompting you to act upon something that is breaking your heart?

- Is anything hindering you from taking action?

Original orphanage home housing 109 kids

Home we moved the kids to. One building for girls & one for boys

Rebecca with the kids at the orphanage in Benin

Tim with Fabrice

Kids carrying the 5- gallon water jugs to get water

"White man no pass" statue at the town entrance

2005 family picture
2004-2006 was the time we were living onboard the Anastasis

CHAPTER 3

"WHITE WOMAN"

"Our life of poverty is as necessary as the work itself. Only in heaven will we see how much we owe to the poor for helping us to love God better because of them."

– Mother Teresa

"White woman, white woman! Please help me. I'm hungry; please be my friend," said a street man in his mid-20's. "White woman, I have no food for my children. Please be my friend," chimed in a middle-aged woman. "Please, white woman – give me a job. I have no work; I cannot feed my family. Please help me."

People swarmed me, pointing to the many overwhelming physical ailments they had, pleading for my help to get them on the big white hospital ship we were living on. Many had come to the ship as a last resort to rescue them from their life-threatening illnesses such as infectious growths, skin eruptions covering their bodies and disease complications I was not even trained to identify. Thousands of Liberian people had already been screened by the seven doctors on board the ship. The small crowd surrounding me was made up of the ones who had missed their chance to be seen by a doctor in order to determine whether they were a candidate for surgery or not. The appointment cards given to those approved for surgery are like golden tickets in these parts of Africa. More than 600 surgery slots had already been given out during the screening days.

In 2005, Liberia was not on my list of first choices for our family to live in, especially since it was only a year and a half after their 14-year civil war had ended. Yet our commitment to Mercy Ships at that time was what brought us to the nation. It was a time when 83% of the population was unemployed. Fifty percent of the population was under the age of 18, and 70% were illiterate. Liberia's brutal civil war had destroyed the nation's economy and displaced over a third of the population. Hospitals, libraries and schools were ravished in the process. The World Health Organization (WHO) reports that in 1989, Liberia had 800 practicing doctors. By the end of the war, it had 50.

In the first couple of weeks in Liberia, I was completely overwhelmed by the sheer needs and desperation of these African people. Each day I would dread having to go off the ship for fear of facing the ones I felt I could not help in any way. Furthermore, I didn't believe that anything I could do would make any real difference in their lives. Their problems were just too big and complicated. The people who were begging on the streets numbered in the hundreds at that time. The ones lined up at the port entrance desperately wanted a response from me as I would pass by; but I didn't even know what to say.

I would say my prayers for them nightly, but that was the extent of what I felt I could do for those off the ship. My job was Renovations Secretary, and my main focus at that time was to get our department ready for the shipyard in South Africa in just a few months. This was a yearly maintenance time for the ship to be taken out of the water and worked on from the inside out, structurally and cosmetically.

Not long after arriving in Liberia, I read a book called *African Friends and Money Matters*. The author talked about how everything in Africa is based upon relationships. To be successful in Africa, it is important to spend a lot of time building friendships and relationships with the nationals if you truly want to affect real change in their nation.

Through that book, I was particularly interested in what the author shared regarding the beggars. When someone is begging, of course they want their needs to be met, but even more than that, they want to be heard and valued for who they are as an individual. One way to come to terms with this dynamic is to consider they may want a friendship with you. Yes, part of it is that they hope to get help financially, but you valuing who they are as a person is even more important to them than money, according to the author. He advised looking the person who is begging in the eyes and asking his or her name, asking them about their lives, families, etc. – truly showing value and worth to them. After this type of encounter, you will have gained a good friend.

While reading this, I started to get excited. I had been so frustrated at how overwhelmed I was each time I had to face the people hanging out on the streets. It became so bad that I didn't even want to go off the ship any more. Emotionally, it was too much. However, after reading this newfound information, I felt personally challenged to test this out and push myself to let the African people teach me a few things. It was time to put myself in the learning role with the ones who terrified me emotionally. My prayer was that God would give me wisdom with each person who came into my path–specifically with those who were begging.

Putting a plan together, I decided that twice a week I would go off the ship for two hours in the morning and just hang out at the end of the port where crowds of people spent most of their day. I would make up my work on the ship in the evening. My plan was to go with no agenda except to learn from them. I would be open to whatever God prompted my heart to do with each person in front of me.

So this is how my Liberian adventure began: "White woman, white woman! Be my friend. Come here," said a woman in her mid- 50's sitting on the side of the dock. I walked over to her and looked her in the eyes and asked what her name was. "My name is Lucia," she replied. "Nice to meet you, Lucia." I said. "My name is Rebecca and yes, I will be your friend." I sat next to her and asked her about her life. After talking for about ten minutes, we made arrangements to meet again the following week at the same time and same place.

Walking to the other end of the port, I was bombarded by all the usual street beggars and sick people. They were ones who did not get an appointment to have surgery on the ship for a variety of reasons.

The sick people were the ones that I felt I needed to address first. They had been told to go home by the port security, and they were very discouraged and confused. I asked different ones what their needs were. One by one, I realized that many had come from hours upcountry with their last hope for treatment doused when they found out the surgery schedule was full. All of the Mercy Ships staff members were told what to look for physically if someone fit the criteria for a surgery – a large tumor, hernia or fistula, or even eye cataracts. I knew there were a few surgery slots saved for the end of our time, so I always kept my radar up for those ones who may come into my path who fit those type of slots and could possibly still see a doctor for assessment.

As I gave them my attention, some began to cry as they told me their concerns. A pleading family member was always by their side, begging me to bring them on the ship. I was caught off guard by the sheer desperation of so many in such hopeless situations. My heart broke, and I began to weep with them as I realized only God could intervene and help them in their ailments. I also knew that some of them might not even make it home alive, as they had come from such distances. One old woman had huge sores all over her body. Another woman had a huge dissented stomach and looked severely jaundiced. A middle-aged man was very frail and boney, possibly with complications from AIDS.

I took a deep breath and asked them all to listen very closely. They huddled close in sheer anticipation of what I would tell them. With tears in my eyes and a lump in my throat, I shared with all of them how valuable each one of them was in God's sight. I told them how incredibly loved they are by God and by us. "That is why we have come to Liberia," I explained. Yet their situations were ones that we could not help on the ship. Many had different diseases which were not curable or treatable. Through my tears, I told them that the only hope we have in these situations is in God our Maker. We serve the God who created us and who has the power to heal, so all we could do was pray for healing. I also explained that some of them might need to prepare to die and to meet God in Heaven very soon, if God would choose not to bring healing to their bodies at this time. "We have to trust God with this," I told them. I encouraged them to make sure that they were ready to meet their Maker and that they were in a right relationship with God. I emphasized that this was the single most important thing they would ever do in their lifetime.

As they were huddled close to me, I stretched my arms out over them and prayed healing, comfort, restoration and salvation for each one. While praying, different ones dropped to the ground and began to raise their hands up toward Heaven and cry. It wasn't deep, loud cries of mourning, but gentle cries of what I felt was them releasing their sicknesses to God. This was the most emotionally difficult thing to witness, yet at the same time, the most precious and amazing thing to be a part of. Through this whole ordeal, the people on the street were looking on in wonder, trying to figure out what this was all about. Whenever you have a group gathered on the streets in Liberia, whoever is near gathers around just to see what is going on. With astronomically-high unemployment, you have hundreds of thousands of people with nothing to do but to watch and get into each other's business. So the crowd around me was getting bigger by the moment.

At the end of the prayer, I encouraged different ones to go to the local hospital to try and get help. It was worth a shot for some of them. The sick ones dispersed and went their separate ways. Noticing a very old, wrinkled woman and her grandson who did not leave, I asked them why they weren't going on their way. The old woman shared with me that they had spent all their money just to get there, and they didn't know anyone in the city, so they had no way to get home. I discretely put five dollars in the woman's hand and kissed her cheek. She grabbed me and hugged me tightly, thanking me over and over. They then hailed a taxi and left.

As I made my way down the street, it was time for the next onslaught of onlookers. "White woman, white woman! Help me; I have no front teeth. Please be my friend," said the man in his mid-20's, who I recognized as a person I had seen on the streets before. I looked him in the eye and asked him his name. "My name is Moses. Will you be my friend?" "Yes, I will," I told him.

"Be my friend too," said the lady sitting on a bench, who I noticed had been watching me intently from the moment I came into her territory. She sold cold water at the end of the pier daily from sun up to sun down. She would rent an old, cracked bucket for five cents a day and wrap cold-water packets around a wool blanket to keep the water cool.

I sat down next to her and said, "Of course I will be your friend." As was becoming the usual custom, I asked her name. "I am Rose. What is your name?" I told her my name and she took my arm right away and started stroking my white skin up and down, inspecting every part intently. I had a hard time understanding her Liberian Kreyol: a melodious version of English. It sounded so strong and broken to me, so Moses would chime into our conversation regularly to help me understand her.

Many others came and surrounded me, all wanting to ask something of me. Rose was extremely aggressive with them and made it clear that today I was her friend, and they needed to go away. I politely told her that she could be nicer to these people and that I would be coming out there two times each week. I would continue to be her friend, but I would also be a friend to those around her.

Twice a week, over the course of almost a year, I was able to build some amazing friendships on the streets. This was a priceless time of learning about this fascinating culture and Liberian life. Those people became my bodyguards, cultural advisers and dear friends. I absolutely fell in love with them.

Moses's story was one of loss and heartache. He really had no idea how old he was. We guessed he was in his mid-20's. He was separated from his family as a young boy during the war and raised himself on the streets. He had heard his parents were dead, yet he longed to be reconnected to his relatives. The hard part was that he had no idea where he would ever find them. He had such a heart to do what was right but just had no direction or genuine care or guidance from anyone. He had formed some very bad habits on the streets and had to do things he was not proud of to survive. He and I instantly became good friends, and this was the beginning of his transformation.

Through our friendship and God's intervention, Moses has completely changed his life. After we ended our service with Mercy Ships, we hired him full-time one year later when we returned to Liberia to start Orphan Relief and Rescue. He has made a strong commitment to God and has become a man of integrity. He regularly tells me that God, through our friendship, rescued him from a hard and awful life on the streets. I have to give a lot of credit to our field team in Liberia, who have been mentoring him in life and his walk with God. They have poured hours into this dear friend. He was also able to get two false teeth put in the front of his mouth, so he can now be proud of his smile. It's certainly an improvement from the gaping hole I saw when I first met him!

Recently, while helping build an orphanage upcountry with our staff, he found some of his relatives. This was a great celebration for them. He found out many family matters that had been such a mystery to him for all those years, including that he is 29 years old. He gives all the credit to God for his new life.

Rose's story was also a tragic one. She lost her husband early on in the war. To feed her four kids she would sell herself to men, like many women do in those circumstances. Prostitution was a common way for a widow to survive through the war and recent post-war days. She made a small amount of money selling cold water but frequently fell back on what she knew would bring in quick cash. Through our friendship, I was able to mentor her in a whole new way of life. I also helped her expand her business to sell soda pop as well as cold water by providing a large ice chest for her.

She heard about a God that loves her and wants to be her lover and friend for life. She claimed to know God when we met, so we just started from there. She often prayed with me about many things in her life, and I would pull her in to pray for others around her as well. On my visit with her in

December 2009, she informed me that she had purchased a piece of property as the first step to building her house. She said she was trying to make me proud. "Next time you see me Rebecca, I will have a house. You will see." I, of course, could not have been more proud of her.

Lucia's past was equally full of tragedy and hardship. But she also had some amazing miracle stories of God's faithfulness in her life. Lucia is a woman who loves God with all her heart. She credits her survival in the war to God's grace and mercy. Her husband abandoned her at the beginning of the war, fleeing for his life to another country. She was left as a single parent with four small children during the most dangerous time of the civil war. Men were considered the largest threat to both the rebel groups as well as the government army and were hunted and decapitated for no reason other than that they posed a threat to each side. So her husband, as well as many other men, fled to neighboring countries as soon as they could to save their own lives. Lucia was from the tribe that the rebels were looking to wipe out and kill. (If you have seen the movie "Hotel Rwanda" you will understand the tribal war tragedies that happen in Africa.) She had to run and hide on a daily basis with all four children. The stories she told me of their survival brought me to tears regularly.

One story she shared was when they had to go through a military checkpoint. She said you never knew if the rebels had taken over these checkpoints or not, so it was always a very scary thing for them. As they approached the guards, she realized they had killed a man from her tribe just ahead of her. This immediately alerted her that the rebel group that ran this checkpoint was out to kill them as well. She told her kids not to say a word. She knew that if they spoke even one word, their tribal tone would be recognized and the guards would shoot to kill immediately. She had seen this happen time and time again. The woman in front of her was also from her tribe, and she was assuring Lucia that they would be just fine. Lucia turned to her kids and told them if she was shot they should keep walking and not react or show any emotion. They should not even look back at her, for fear they might be identified as her children and shot as well. She told them they would have to be strong. As she was retelling this story, tears welled up in her eyes as she remembered this particular event. As a mom listening to this, I was also in tears just hearing what another mother had gone through.

As they walked forward, the woman in front of her was asked a question to which she had to respond. As she did, the guards immediately recognized her dialect and shot her right in front of the group. Due to the distraction of this woman being killed, Lucia and her children were able to keep walking forward, showing no emotion, and through God's miraculous hand of protection they got through the checkpoint without anyone recognizing them as members of the hunted tribe.

Through the years, Lucia has become an amazing and loyal friend to me. No matter what I need, even to this day, she is there for me. I was able to help her start several small businesses, and she has helped me practically with kids, household and mom things. I never imagined these meetings on the street would turn into such rewarding friendships.

While the ship was there, many men who needed jobs would come daily to the entrance of the port begging for work. During each visit to the street, I would tell them that all the jobs were filled already, but we would pray. We would all bow our heads and say a prayer right there. When these men found work, different ones would show up with fruit to say "Thank you for praying. God answered our prayers!" Our family cabin on the ship was always full of fruit.

The Liberian police and United Nations peacekeepers guarding the port security gates began to call me the "Liberian white woman". They watched me constantly, partially to protect me and partially out of curiosity. When people came to the ship for help, particularly in the first couple of months the ship was in port, the guards would send them away as usual. If they did not leave, they would tell them to talk to a Liberian white woman named Rebecca, for she would listen to them. They would never be let into the port where the ship was docked, but some would wait for hours just to talk to me at the port entrance.

I started making my walks in the evening after dinner to the end of the port, just to make sure no one was waiting for me into the night. The guards would always tell me when someone was waiting. The number of sick people showing up to the port decreased as time went on. Many would get word that the surgery slots were filled and no more appointments were available. So this became a lot more manageable as the months went by.

The guards would thank me daily for loving their people. They would say, "Rebecca, we are always watching you, and we know you love us Liberians so much." I would always reply to them that I did love them so much, but God loved them even more than I ever could. These guards also became my very good friends. I would often pray with them about different needs in their lives as well.

The list of stories where God transformed people's lives through showing them value and worth is endless. As I write this, **I am still amazed thinking back to how my naivety caused me to walk in such fear and almost kept miracles from being accomplished in others' lives. Through knowledge and just being teachable and walking in humility, God converted this fear in my life into transformational miracles for others.**

Through my time on the streets, I fell in love with the Liberian people and Africans in general. God broke my heart for the lost, abandoned, destitute, sick and hurting people right in front of me. I learned about culture, world-view and how Africans think on those streets.

This was priceless training ground for the future service God would ask my husband and me to join Him in. This also taught me how not to walk forward in fear when I did not understand things in these different countries. God is right there with us and will give us wisdom on how to walk forward if we just ask. We are not alone in these endeavors. Our job is to just be available and teachable.

These are some things I learned about my precious friends on the streets of Liberia:

- They each have an amazing story of survival from the civil war and have suffered great personal loss.

- They each have enormous pain they are carrying that only God can heal.

- They each have so many tangible needs that are so individualized, and only through friendship will you find out what these are and what can be done to restore their dignity.

- They want and need a friend that will accept them where they are and love them for who they are.

- They do not want to be looked down upon. They don't want your pity, but they do need your mercy.

- Once people get a glimpse of their worth, they soar.

It makes no difference who it is or where they are from. It could be the people on the streets of Seattle or all the way in Africa. It could be children in foster care here in the U.S. or in an orphanage setting abroad, in a business situation, in a nursing home, or even someone in your own home. It doesn't matter where these people are; if they feel abandoned and discarded from society, they need to understand that their life matters. They need to feel love and acceptance. If they feel that from you, then they will be apt to listen to the guidance you give in helping them to help themselves through the hope and encouragement they receive.

No one wants to be judged. People repel judgment. As we value them through Christ's love, listen to them, care for them and try to understand them, we can have a genuinely positive effect on their life. The inwardly dead can come alive. They can feel a renewed hope and excitement for life with no more fear of the present or future, no more fear of living or dying.

Questions for Personal Reflection:

- What is a big fear in your life?

- What are some things that will help you overcome this fear?

- If there is nothing in it for you, are you willing to give out of yourself for the sake of another person?

CHAPTER 4

THE UNEXPECTED

"Hungry for love, He looks at you. Thirsty for kindness, He begs of you. Naked for loyalty, He hopes in you. Homeless for shelter in your heart, He asks of you. Will you be that one to Him?"

— *Mother Teresa*

After the dry-docking and shipyard repairs in October of 2005, we prepared for the twelve-day sail back to Liberia. It was a difficult thing for me – through previous ocean voyages I had learned that my body did not endure sailing well. Twelve days were going to be a real challenge.

We had been ported in Cape Town, South Africa for over six weeks doing a promotional tour after our dry-dock time was over. Daily public tours were going on as we were filling up the ship with supplies for our return to Liberia for a ten-month field service.

We had a five-star birthing spot overlooking Cape Town's famous Table Mountain, as well as amazing shopping and entertainment plazas with breathtaking views all around. This is a beautiful resort area where tourists from all over the world come to vacation.

Thinking of going back to Liberia (one of the poorest nations in the world) was tiring. I was excited to see my Liberian friends again, but I just did not feel quite ready to

...at harsh environment once more, not to mention the long sail to get there.

Three days before leaving South Africa, I asked God what I could do to prepare myself personally for Liberia. I needed something to look forward to. I did not like that I dreaded going back. After this simple prayer, the thought came to my mind very strongly that I was to buy food for all my Liberian friends who had no jobs and had to go out each day looking for food for their families. I processed this with my husband, and we agreed with our small budget that we would spend $100 on bags of beans and rice. Little did I know this idea would be the start of an entirely new adventure.

The next day, as I was headed off the gangway to buy the food at a local Cape Town store, I ran into Tim and another gentleman from Switzerland named Pierre, with whom Tim had just eaten lunch. Pierre was a retired man volunteering in our renovations department for three weeks. He had been a banker for 30 years in Switzerland and wanted to use his retirement years to help others. He was kind, yet very direct and vocal about what was on his mind. He pulled me aside to tell me that Tim had shared with him that I was going to buy food for my Liberian friends and that he wanted to pitch in. He said he wanted me to buy as much food as I could fit on the ship and that he would pay for it. He said there was no limit.

I was a bit caught off guard by this, and I asked him to please give me some sort of amount that he had in mind. He continued to just say, "As much as you can fit on the ship." I told him I needed to think about this to see how we could manage buying a large quantity of food before we sailed in less than 48 hours. I knew I would need to get the captain's approval for what amount he would actually allow me to bring on the ship, and that would depend on what space was available.

After talking with the captain, I was authorized to go ahead with the plan as long as I worked with the cargo hold men to see how much we could actually get on board. So, after making all their assessments of space, they gave me the okay to bring three to five pallets of food on board. The only catch was that I had to get it to the port before 10 the next morning for the final loading of supplies before we sailed – and it was already 5 p.m. In my mind, I could not even imagine this possibly working, but I was sure willing to try.

At this point all of our vehicles were being loaded on the ship, and there were no local stores that could handle what I wanted to do. I breathed a prayer to God and asked Him to provide for this food to get on the ship and give me wisdom about how to do this. As I said this prayer, I grabbed my little purse and headed off the gangway, not even knowing where to start. My thought was to walk to the little grocery store nearby and ask them some questions about where they bought their food. Yet even this seemed crazy with my time being so short.

As I headed off the gangway, I saw one of our local vendors, David, who had helped us get all our renovation supplies on board, pulling away from our dock in his car. Just two hours prior, I had given David a small thank-you gift and said my good-bye to him.

David was a very kind and gentle man, always deep in thought, yet ready to serve. Our renovations hold was filled and ready for the sail back to Liberia thanks to this man. As I waved another goodbye to him from a distance, I saw him turn his car around and drive over to me. He rolled down his window and said, "I know all your cars are loaded for the sail, and you look like you have somewhere to go. Do you need a ride?" I proceeded to tell him my situation, and he immediately lit up as I was talking. He said, "Get in, Rebecca. I know exactly where you need to go."

He took me to the perfect place, a food warehouse twenty-five minutes away. This warehouse was strictly for vendors, and he had a membership card to get in. If I were to have planned it myself, I could not have done any better than I did with David's help. He told me what a privilege it was for him to be a part of all this. While I was there, I picked out five pallets of food, already packed with plastic. Each pallet was about four feet wide by five feet tall. One contained beans, one rice, one maize, one lentils and one a hearty dried soup mix. This was enough for thousands of families to have a meal. David negotiated a discount with the owner, who was also excited to be a part of the process.

I came back to the ship and worked out the details with the cargo guys, who reiterated the need to have the food there by 10 a.m.; David spent all evening arranging a truck to donate his time and services to pick up the food and deliver it to the ship the next morning before we sailed. David was a true instrument of God's hands to make this all possible. The total food bill was quite large, yet Pierre said it was his pleasure to pay for it.

After all this food was on board that evening, I was in total awe of what God had done. For some reason God wanted this food on board the ship, and He took our meager hundred-dollar idea and turned it into five pallets of food! My eyes flooded with tears as I lay in bed that night in absolute awe of God. I then had so much anticipation and excitement to see what God was going to do with all this food!

I should mention that Mercy Ships does not distribute food; they don't want to create dependency in this area and many other excellent organizations specialize in these services. The CEO of the ship told me to keep this under our personal mercy ministry endeavors. This was not a normal Mercy Ship thing; they made an exception in this case because of the donation given.

I never realized the impact that simple food distributing would have on a country in which the majority of people go out every day looking for food for their families. The food that was donated in South Africa was distributed to some very poor villages in Liberia. Different people on board were a part of this process, and we were able to give over 900 families a bag of food for Christmas. Some of these people had hardly anything to feed their families. These were villages where people had just moved back after being in IDP (Internally Displaced Person) camps for years during the civil war. They had just recently gone back to their own land to find nothing left from when they lived there. They had to completely rebuild again. So this food was such a welcome gift.

One lady was in the woods picking greens because she had nothing to feed her family that day. When given a bag of food, she broke down and cried. When she finally got her emotions under control, she said that no one had ever given her anything like that before. She kept saying over and over, "Thank you. Thank you. Thank you." The gratefulness of all those who received this food was so rewarding.

We knew that food distribution was only a temporary measure to help people, but what it did show was that they were not forgotten. In a land where human life is not valued due to many years of war and death, this also showed people how valuable they are to us, as well as to God. I loved to tell them the story of how we got the food in South Africa and that God was thinking of them way in advance. It was no accident that we got five pallets of food onboard right before the ship sailed.

Many orphans and widows also benefited from this food. While we stumbled across the hungry children in the orphanage homes and began to feed them, God prompted our hearts to get involved with them in a greater capacity. God used this food as a tool to begin building relationships with the poorest of the poor. Our eyes were opened to many more needs that God wanted us to see. This was the beginning of something more than just food!

During the sail back to Liberia, Tim and I became good friends with Pierre. We saw this retired man in his 60's wanting to make a huge difference in others' lives with the latter years of his own life. Through our friendship, we shared with him about the orphanage we had just helped in Benin, and he got excited about personally seeing the kids in the near future. We planned to fly back to Benin to check on the children while we were still in Liberia, so Pierre decided he would meet us there during our visit. After about five months in Liberia, we flew back to Benin. This time with Pierre sealed our hearts together in the endeavor to make sure these children would have a future.

While on that trip to Benin, the social welfare workers began to ask us if we would consider building a new orphanage in their area. They said this was the greatest need in their town because of the number of orphans who come into their system on a regular basis. We clearly understood this was a great need and promised to prayerfully consider it. Even with these discussions, it was difficult to imagine a new orphanage becoming a reality any time soon.

When Pierre went back to Switzerland after spending time with the children in Benin, he continued to keep them close to his heart. As he would share their story, others' hearts were broken for the plight of these children as well.

Not long after this trip, I got a phone call from Pierre saying that something wonderful had just happened. An elderly woman had just donated a large sum of money for the children in Benin. He said, "I will email you all the details. I am completely speechless by what this woman has done."

This email came from him that day:

Recently I invited a few ladies for lunch at my home in Switzerland. A woman (who we will call Yvonne) was present. During lunch I mentioned my time with the ship as well as the children's home we helped in Benin. The purpose of this lunch was not to talk about my work in Africa, but was just a friendly meeting talking about Jesus.

A few days later a member of her church called me and asked me if I could go and see Yvonne at her flat. She didn't tell me why.

Yvonne lives in a one-bedroom apartment with a small pension. When she was 17 years old she left France to escape the Nazi persecution. She worked in a monastery near Fribourg (Switzerland) for eight years without pay. Work was hard, but she enjoyed it. She had plenty to eat, and it was a good life, she said.

As she left Fribourg after the war was over, the head Priest asked her to accept an amount of money for the work she had done. She didn't expect such a gift, but was told that everybody who works was entitled to a salary.

When I arrived at her place, 50,000 Swiss Franc were on the dining table (equal to about $40,000 US). I was confused to see such a large sum of money in cash. She told me that throughout all these years she kept the money. It was now time to give back part of it to a good cause.

"I have plenty, she said. "Please accept this gift, as I have a real desire to help these children in Africa, and you must take this for them. I have discussed this issue with my church and my decision is made. Please don't say no."

Well, I did say no, because basically I felt I could not accept such a gift from her. It was not appropriate. She then said, "Don't worry. My church will look after me should I leave this place." I finally agreed to take the money for the orphans. She keeps active by serving lunch twice a week in a retirement home nearby her flat.

I can only say that I have witnessed a real act of love. This act has kept me from sleeping for days.

With this gift, Pierre decided to use her finances towards building a permanent orphanage/safe home for the children in Benin. This is now fully built thanks to a sweet, selfless woman and a retired gentleman who wanted to make a difference for others in their lifetime. It reminds me of the story in the Bible where the widow gave her last coin.

This miracle home for the children in Benin, West Africa, was finished in October 2008. The children who are orphans in this very needy area up north now have a permanent safe place to go when they come into the system. The Mayor actually donated the land on which this new home was built.

Without their knowledge they picked February 14, 2009, Valentine's Day in America, as the community open house and celebration of their new home. God revealed to me the symbolism of this being an American day to celebrate the loved ones in our lives. He was making a statement of His love for these hurting children on this day. They are so valuable to Him. My eyes still well up with tears as God's redemption story unfolds in these precious lives. This day of love extends far into the heavenly realm. The children were all dressed in their new matching African outfits. There was food, singing, dancing and overall celebration of God's miracle for them on this eventful day.

A good friend of ours from a western nation accepted full ownership and leadership of this new home. Since she was educated and spiritually strong, we knew she would do a wonderful job raising these children. Another wonderful woman was also brought in to be the 'mama' of the home and to live in the orphanage full-time. The children are being taught a whole new value system. Learning about an incredible God of love who created them to be unique and valuable is transformational. I know beyond a doubt that God is always in pursuit of a personal relationship with them.

Once the new orphanage home was completed, we told the social welfare workers only to bring us the children who had no father or mother living and those whom they cry over knowing the conditions they lived in. In many parts of Africa, and many developing nations around the world, it is a sad fact that some children in orphanages are not true orphans. Their family has no means to feed another mouth, so in desperation they will either abandon their children or bring them directly to a nearby orphanage, hoping and praying for a better life for them in an institutionalized setting. So even though their need is great, we felt our focus was meant to be on those who had truly lost both parents.

The social welfare office immediately had 30 children picked out for us from a nearby village. When we picked up the first fifteen children, with the commitment to pick up the next fifteen the following week, our friend had her first opportunity to truly show her skills with the kids. It was very evident from the start that she was the right woman for the job.

When we brought the first group of children home, they were very scared and didn't know how to react to this amazing new place where they were going to live. Their relatives had dressed them up quite nicely to make a good impression on us as we were picking them up. For one reason or another, the relatives did not want to keep the children and were all too eager to give them over to our care.

To ease their anxiety and fears, we gathered them around the dining room table to get to know them a bit before taking them to their rooms. I began by asking them different questions through my French translator, Pastor Roland.

I started with the question of what they did for fun each day. As we went around to each child, one by one they mentioned what chores they did in the home where they had lived. One said she took care of the babies in the home.

Another was in charge of fetching water all day. Another cleaned and cooked. Another hauled charcoal and wood. As we kept going around the table, I felt like Pastor Roland must not be asking the right question, as I was trying to get them to talk about what they liked to do for fun, not what their chores were.

I stopped Pastor Roland and said, "Pastor, I do not think the kids understand my question. I am thinking that we need to ask this question a little differently to find out what they do for fun." He said, "No, I am asking the right question. They understood me correctly." Confused, I asked, "Then why are they all listing the chores they do and not mentioning things like playing games, singing, dancing, etc.?" Pastor Roland looked at me, a bit in distress, and then he briskly walked to the other side of the room. At this point I was really confused. I watched him lean over a small table with his head hung low as if he wasn't feeling too well.

Suddenly I was left with all fifteen children's eyes on me, none of us knowing what was going on with Pastor Roland. I was helpless because he was also my voice. I thought maybe he was sick, or maybe I had just unintentionally offended him. I walked over to Pastor and tapped him on his shoulder, asking if he was okay. As he looked up at me, he was sobbing and not able to even speak. This caught me completely off guard, due to the well-composed countenance of this man. He had never cried before in my presence, and I could not imagine what was causing him to be so shaken up now.

When I asked him if he needed some time alone, he made it clear that he just needed a minute and would get it together. After about five minutes, I tapped him again and said, "Okay, Pastor. Please tell me what has brought on such emotion, and please tell me if I have done something to offend you."

He very graciously looked up at me, still with tears dripping down his face, and said, "Rebecca, you have no idea where these kids have really come from. They are all dressed well, and the relatives worked hard to give you a good impression of themselves as caretakers, but the reality is that these kids were slaves in these homes. I did ask them the right question, but these kids do not have fun. They were just servants to their relatives, and they worked from sun-up to sun-down to earn their keep in those homes." He went on to tell me that when he was eight, he too became an orphan and was raised by many different relatives.

He said that as an orphan in many parts of Africa, even if you live with a relative, you become the servant of that home. You do not have special treatment. You have to earn your own way. He said that he did not have a childhood; he had to serve everyone in his relatives' home. If he did anything wrong, he would be beaten. He barely had anything to eat and was never able to rest. As he shared this, he was very emotional, remembering his own childhood as an orphan. He looked me straight in the eyes and said, "Rebecca, what you people are doing for these kids is a rescue mission. You are rescuing them from a life of slavery. I want to thank you for what you are doing for our people. These children will now have a healthy future and a good life because of what you are doing. Please do not be deceived by these children's appearances. They were slaves. And now they are free."

Wow. My heart was overwhelmed at that moment. I actually had been a little disheartened picking these children up that day and seeing that they were so well dressed. From the outside, they looked taken care of. Yet I was looking through my Western view of things and really did not understand the harshness of the life they had actually just been delivered from. The reality began to sink in regarding what we had just done that day. These kids had been rescued from neglect, abuse and slavery!

That same day, the head social welfare officer of that area looked at us and said, "Can I please bring you more orphans? We have so many in our community, and I can get you 100 more tomorrow if you want them. As many as you can handle I will get you, and these will be children with no mother and father." I looked at her and explained that we could not take those kinds of numbers at this point. "We are starting small and, through the year, we will bring in more. But at this home, we will not have capacity for those numbers." She looked at me and said, "Okay, but please do not forget about the many more orphans in our area who are living in distressing situations." I promised her we would not forget.

To this day, we continue to be in awe of this new home for the kids who had no mother or father to care for them. On my recent trip to check on them, I was able to stay at the orphanage/safe home where we now have 60 children. Each morning before they ate breakfast and left for school, they would have a time of singing praises to God and a time of praying for their villages. As I lay in my room the first morning after my arrival, too tired to get up that early, I could not believe what I was hearing – in the Voodoo capital of the world, no less! Children, who have come from terrible abuse and neglect, from some of the darkest places on earth, are now praising God. They are being raised to have a heart of compassion for all their people.

The magnitude of what God has already done in each of their lives is unbelievable. The stories some of these children can tell about where they have come from are like an Indiana Jones movie. It is hard to believe all the things these children have gone through in the name of Voodoo. It is very crazy stuff. Some of the children have deep slice marks on their faces and bodies left from tribal rituals they endured. These give us a small glimpse of the life they have come from.

Now, though, they are free and so full of life. **I strongly believe that each child has the keys to change each of their villages, as they are raised as valued individuals through Christ.** They have such a heart for their people, and I look forward to seeing these children go back as world changers in their hometowns, bringing a whole new value system for human life through the knowledge of the God who created each of us equally. Orphaned, diseased, deformed, impoverished or wealthy – we are all the same in God's eyes. Each of us is unique and valuable.

Questions for Personal Reflection:

- What do you need faith for today? Is there something that you need God to come through for?

- In thinking of Yvonne's story, are you willing to surrender your assets and resources to God?

- What steps of faith, however small, can you take towards helping others?

Anastasis ship

Our family on the ship

Newly built orphanage/safe home

Kids on celebration day Feb. 14, 2009

CHAPTER 5

BURDENS PUT TO A MISSION

"When a poor person dies of hunger, it has not happened because God did not take care of him or her. It happened because neither you nor I wanted to give that person what he or she needed."

– Mother Teresa

Mrs. Fatu Smith had resolved that she was willing to die with her 80 orphan children if God did not provide food for them soon. Each morning at 5:00, she and the children would have a prayer time asking God to provide food for them that day. Miraculously, God would, even if just a small amount. They were always thankful.

After years of seeing God provide each day, for some unknown reason, three whole days had gone by with no food. They felt that maybe the inevitable was close at hand.

Huddled beside her children lying on moldy mattresses in their war-torn orphanage home just outside Liberia's capital city of Monrovia, Fatu Smith began to lose hope. As she cried out to God in her personal quiet time, she felt strongly in her heart that she was to ask for help at the big white hospital ship she had heard was docked in Monrovia. She had approached many other organizations and people, yet no one gave her the time of day. She didn't know if this would be any different, but in her desperation she felt she must try.

Fatu Smith was born a Muslim and endured much hardship at a very young age. When she was 14, she was given over by her family to a Muslim man to be one of his wives. She regularly endured horrific abuse physically, sexually and emotionally from this man as a young teenager. After many years of torture, she escaped this harsh life in her early twenties. She was fortunate to then marry a good and honest man, Mr. Sebastion Smith, whom she is still with today.

Stories of war and survival are numerous with this couple, yet a miraculous healing in her body is what she said was her most life-changing experience. She was near death when God miraculously healed her after seven years of physical affliction from stomach ulcers and cancer. After this divine experience, she promised Jesus she would faithfully serve Him and open a charitable institution for orphan children. This was when she established the Divine Healing Ministries to fulfill her promise to Jesus.

She then began to share about Christ in all the villages around her. She even started praying for the sick, and some people were instantly healed. She said her life mission had become serving God and others with her whole heart.

Toward the end of Liberia's 14-year civil war, Fatu began to find children wandering in the jungle, naked and abandoned, with no one to care for them. She would bring them into her home in fulfillment of her promise to God. She took these children in as her own. After several years she had 80 children and seven helpers.

Fatu and her husband Sebastion had been well off financially before the civil war, but they lost it all when the rebels stole and destroyed everything they owned. Sebastion had worked in the investment commissioner's office with the government for 20 years making the equivalent of 50 US dollars a month. He chose not to be corrupt or take bribes and, therefore, could not feed his children. A 100-pound bag of rice was $22 at that time and it would only last three days, so you can imagine the hardship this created.

When Fatu came to the port asking to be let into the gate, the guards turned her down. Not one to be deterred easily, she waited at the port entrance until she saw a Mercy Ships vehicle approaching. Amazingly, this happened to be a vehicle full of people headed to do mercy ministries at an orphanage in Monrovia.

One woman in the vehicle was my friend Jennifer. Fatu immediately began to tell Jennifer of her desperate situation. It was very common to have this happen when leaving the port, but Jennifer said she felt that she really needed to listen closely to what this desperate woman was saying and make sure this woman felt valued.

Jennifer asked her to come back the next day so she could sit down and hear her full story. Jennifer then had the difficult task of politely telling Fatu that we could not help her because the ship was not taking on any new projects. Our time in Liberia was coming to an end, and we were wrapping up all our current projects. We were in the eighth month of our ten-month field service.

Fatu, being so desperate, pleaded with Jennifer to just come and take a look at her children. Out of compassion Jennifer felt compelled to go and see this woman's home. God would use this action to spiral a whole new chain of events, providing for yet another group of vulnerable children.

I asked Jennifer to share her journal writings with me after seeing Fatu's home for the first time. This is what she wrote:

Fatu gave her life to Jesus after He healed her supernaturally. She told Him that she would serve Him always. She opened a home for little ones with no home after the war. She could not stand by and do nothing. When she realized she was unable to care well for these, and they were sick due to their small living quarters, she made the decision to take them in at her own home. This home her and her husband built years ago on their property of one acre. The home was meant for them and their five children.

The house sits in despair, only a shell really. There is no money for paint, ceilings or beds. Food is a real problem. The home now houses 80 children, most of them between two and 13 years old. They don't know where the next meal is coming from. But God is faithful. Somehow, he provides 22 US dollars every third day so a bag of rice can be purchased. That will feed them for three days.

They have a well, but the water can only be used for washing. Drinking water has to be purchased and hauled in by car each day or every other day. The generator is broken so there is no light, and the old refrigerator sits in the corner remembering days gone by when it performed the job it was created to do.

A concrete foundation sits decaying in the hot sun. The plan to build a new dormitory where girls could sleep in one floor and the boys on another has been abandoned due to lack of finances.

Food, water, well, generator, beds, dorms—so many hopes and so many dreams. Are God's arms too short? I think not. I believe He has heard the plea of the persistent woman, and her name is Fatu.

My husband and I went out to dinner with Jennifer and her husband the day she visited Fatu's orphanage home. Her heart was heavy as she was telling me about the orphanage she had just seen. This woman had 80 children that literally had nothing to eat that day. She was able to find enough money in her pockets to get them a large bag of rice so that the children could eat, but she was really concerned for how they would eat after that bag was gone. No one was helping them.

As she was talking, I thought of the full pallet of food from South Africa that I had left in the hold of the ship specifically for these type of needy situations. I told her about the food and asked her if we could just pile a Land Rover with food and take it to these kids. I was sure we could give them at least a couple of months' worth of food. She got all excited as we talked, and we planned our day to head out there.

Of course, when we showed up with a whole Land Rover of food, it was a true miracle. The children and workers were so excited at the sight of this food. They rejoiced and celebrated like it was Christmas. It was quite precious. Fatu said "Oh, we should never doubt God taking care of us! Never, ever doubt God. This is a true miracle. Thank you! Thank you!"

Looking at their living conditions, I saw they were in need of so much for proper sanitation. They had no adequate toilets or showers, their well had been destroyed by the war so they had no drinkable water, and their sleeping quarters were terrible. The children were sleeping on mattresses on the floor that were moldy due to rain leaking in from their main room, which had no roof. The facility they were living in was in desperate need of repair.

I tried to look at this all objectively and was determined not to get emotionally involved. Even though I had a strong love for orphan children, I didn't really want to take on another big orphanage project at this time. I had all my walls of emotional protection up so I wouldn't get sucked in with what I was seeing. I threw out my little comments to God, telling Him that this was just a food delivery and that was it!

I closed my mind to the future of it all – until I picked up one little girl named Gifty. She was about three years old and had scabies, fungus and staph infections all over her skin. I then looked around at all the other kids who also had the same skin ailments. I knew they could be easily treated by a two-dollar medicine. I had just dealt with these same health issues with the kids in Benin. It was not an expensive remedy to bring relief to all the children. In my mind I began to calculate that it would only cost about 160 US dollars to treat them all.

Looking around at the malnourished children, a sobering thought came to me. **What if these were my own biological children and I was dead? What if someone with the power to relieve their pain walked by and saw my babies suffering like this yet chose to do nothing? If possible I would cry from my grave a big, "Shame on you for not helping my babies!"** Tears welled up in my eyes as I felt like God spoke to my heart about the future and destiny that He had for little Gifty in my arms and for each of the other children who are equally precious and dear to His heart.

Sitting close to me were three other very sick little ones – Esther, Joshua and Kou. They were very lethargic and weak. Their skin was the worst I had ever seen. A deep, black fungus was covering their weak little bodies. I felt in my heart they would not live long without immediate medical attention and adequate nutrition in their bodies. Looking closer, I knew that God was prompting me to get involved in this orphanage home and in these kids' lives, just like a mother would. He wanted this to be more than just a food delivery!

That evening in sharing this with Tim, he was quick to say that if God was in it, then I shouldn't try to fight it. Yet, for me, it was a longer struggle. I was counting the cost: my time, the money that would need to be raised and the emotional energy this would take.

The next day I determined that it did not have to be me alone doing the majority of work necessary to help this home. I decided to find an organization that would be more than willing to help these desperate children. There were plenty of non-governmental organizations in the country after the civil war, and there were plenty of relief agencies. Surely this was the exact type of need they were looking to address. Many of the organizations there are ones we are familiar with here in America, so I started making phone calls. With each call my heart would sink as the person on the other side would say, "Oh, I am so sorry, but that home is not on our certified list of orphanages. Therefore we cannot help them. Helping homes like that will create dependency, and many are already corrupt, so we cannot help them in any way. Unless the government certifies them as being a credible orphanage, we won't touch them."

I could not believe my ears. I would ask a bunch of questions but got the same response over and over. They would each say the same thing. "If you can get them up to a certified state with the government, then we may be able to put them on our list for assistance." I thought about how unfair this was for the homes that had amazing directors yet no resources to help their children. How could they get up to certified conditions if no one would help them? I understood that many were corrupt and using the Westerners as a resource, but what about ones such as Fatu and Sebastion Smith, who had amazing references and had proven themselves with their whole community to be honest leaders?

To be certified, I found out that the orphanage had to have a well with fresh drinking water. They had to have showers and working toilets. The children had to be sleeping off the floor and all be enrolled in school. This seemed impossible without outside intervention – especially after a devastating war where so many people lost everything.

That evening as I listened to a CD that Rick Warren (author of *Purpose Driven Life*) spoke on, these words pierced my heart: **"When God gives you a burden, don't ignore it. Feed it, and let it break your heart. That is God's heart. Don't stuff or ignore those burdens."** Tears welled up in my eyes, and I knew again what God was asking.

Within a few days, I submitted a proposal to Mercy Ships and told them that I would raise all the finances for this project if they would allow me to take it on. The ship we were on was being taken out of service in a matter of months, so my position as renovations secretary was phasing out. Because of these circumstances, I was given special permission to pursue the project. The leadership team stressed that it was my sole responsibility to raise the money for this project – the ship's budget for previously planned projects had already been stretched beyond the limit. I agreed to those terms and then began to put my plea out to our dear friends and family.

In six weeks $27,000 was raised, and these kids were given a whole new life. We started with food and medicine, and we completely renovated their orphanage home. My husband encouraged his renovations team to come out and help accomplish this task on their days off. He was even able to give me two men from his department in a greater capacity as their jobs allowed. My husband, along with a man named Matt Le Page and a Liberian named Morris provided the backbone for the success of the project. We also hired 20 Liberians to work on this project, as the ship would be leaving Liberia soon and we needed this done very quickly. Some of the men we hired were ones I had met on the streets. It was so rewarding to see some of my established friends working with us. Feeding the families of my friends from the street, by giving them a job, was just another bonus I did not expect in this whole ordeal.

Matt Le Page and I learned that we worked really well together, as he was the structural engineer who coordinated the workers and showed them what to do, and I was the visionary for the project. Morris was our skilled national who was equally priceless in directing us culturally and leading the workers through honesty and integrity issues as they worked with us. Many co-workers and friends also got involved, which became a great partnership with many who had a heart to help. Because of the generosity of so many, these children got a new lease on life. They were given a new well, new showers, toilets, a new roof, plastered walls, bunk beds, as well as new flooring.

A year later, when we came back as Orphan Relief and Rescue, we were able to add a school building onto the back of the home, a large boy's dormitory, security fence, more latrines/toilets, showers, and many more bunk beds with mosquito nets. We are also currently helping them start some small businesses and operating our Child Development Program to help bring up these children to become healthy and whole adults.

At the end of the construction project, we asked the social welfare office to send their workers out to certify this orphanage home so that Fatu would be eligible for other organizations to help her with food and medicine. As the welfare workers walked through the home, they were so impressed. They said this was the second best orphanage home in all of Liberia that was not being run by a non-governmental organization.

The welfare workers began to plead with me not to leave their country and forget about the other needy children in homes with equally terrible conditions. One of them, with tears in his eyes, said, "I have a list of 79 more orphanages in the same conditions that you found this one in, and no one is helping them either. Please do not leave. So many children are in such desperate need. I go home and cry at night because of what I see every day. It is all so horrible, and no one will touch these. Please help us." I repeated his words in my mind. *79,* I thought. *Oh my, that is a crazy amount in need.*

After the social welfare workers left, Fatu asked if she could rename the orphanage in my name to honor my intervention to resurrect the dying home. I quickly declined the offer and let her know that this was her vision with God, not mine. I told her my hope was for others to take up helping her where we left off, now that she had a certified home. I personally had no plans to return to Liberia. Fatu, being a very spiritual person, then spoke directly to me. She said, "Rebecca, when you return to America you will form an organization to help orphanages not only in Liberia but also in all of Africa." I looked at her and just smiled, with no plans like that for the future. My thoughts were solely on having closure with Africa at that point.

Her husband Sebastion then joined us and asked if he could also speak to me before we said our good-byes. Our time on the ship was coming to a close, and Tim had gone home to America a month before our departure from Mercy Ships to prepare for our arrival. He was not there to share in these conversations, but he was equally thanked for all his work.

Sebastion said "Rebecca, we want you to know what this help has meant to us personally as directors of this home. You already know that this was a rescue mission for these kids, but we also want you and your husband and all the workers who came from Mercy Ships to know that this was a rescue mission for us as parents of these children." Fatu interjected and started crying as she explained how difficult it was, as parents of the children, to watch the incredible suffering these kids had gone through. She sobbed and sobbed as she talked about hearing the children cry themselves to sleep at night because their little bellies were empty. She explained that, as a mom, it was awful to know she could not do anything to alleviate their suffering.

Then Sebastion interrupted and said "I am not going to cry like my wife is, but I so want you and your husband to know what this has meant to me as a man." He began to tell me how he had worked faithfully for the government for over 20 years, choosing not to be dishonest or take bribes. He also taught in the evenings at the university, but this only brought in a meager income. In spite of working so hard during days and evenings, he still was not able to feed his family.

Then the tears started to run down his face, and he began to just sob, barely able to speak because he was crying so much. He kept trying to wipe away his tears and talk. He also explained that seeing the hungry and sick children all around him was a very shameful thing because it made him feel like he could not provide for his own home.

He had to take breaks from talking because the tears and emotions were too overwhelming for him as he described all this. Through his tears, my emotions began to come to the surface, too. I could sense the tremendous pain he had to go through, and my heart broke as I watched this strong man fall apart as he recalled the humiliation of poverty and suffering that he had experienced as a man and as a provider.

When he composed himself enough to talk again, he said "Rebecca, what you people have done for us has now brought dignity back to me as a man and as a father. I can stand tall now with no shame. If I die tonight, I would die with dignity and peace. You have truly restored my manhood." He began to choke up so much he could not speak anymore. Through his tears, he kept saying over and over, "Thank you. Thank you."

As he was talking, I knew this was not just small talk; this was deep pain that was being set free through this miracle in their life. What they both shared deeply affected me.

When they were done sharing, I told them that this was God's doing, and God's miracle that we all got to be a part of. "So please thank God, not me," I said. Sebastion looked me square in the eyes and said, "Rebecca, I agree that this was God's miracle of provision and yes, we are thanking God so much for this. But for this miracle to happen it took someone to say 'yes'. And you, Rebecca, said 'yes'. So thank you."

Through his tears and words, God gently spoke to my heart that I was to listen very closely to what he was saying and let this concept go very deep into my heart. God is waiting for His people to say "yes".

I let myself imagine what conditions these kids would be in if we did not help them. It was a very awful realization that some of them may have already been dead without our intervention, or they would still be alive but suffering greatly. I later came across something that Mother Teresa wrote that brought home this reality about our responsibility to help those in our path.

When a poor person dies of hunger, it has not happened because God did not take care of him or her. It happened because neither you nor I wanted to give that person what he or she needed. We have refused to be instruments of love in the hands of God to give the poor a piece of bread, to offer them a dress with which to ward off the cold. It has happened because we did not recognize Christ when, once more he appeared under the guise of pain, identified with a man numb from the cold, dying of hunger, when he came in a lonely human being, in a lost child in search of a home.

This made me think of what Jesus stated in Matthew 25: 25-46: *"For I was hungry, and you gave Me something to eat; I was thirsty, and you gave Me drink; I was a stranger and you invited me in; Naked, and you clothed me, I was sick and you visited me, I was in prison, and you came to me. Then the righteous will answer Him, saying 'Lord when did we see you hungry and feed you, or thirsty and give you drink? And when did we see you a stranger, and invite you in, or naked and clothed you? And when did we see you sick, or in prison, and came to you?' And the King will answer and say to them, "Truly I say to you to the extent that you did it to one of these brothers of mine, even to the least of them, you did it to me. '"*

In these places I am finding Jesus present. Through relationship and individual stories of poverty and hardship, my heart has gone to a level of love and compassion I did not know could exist outside of Heaven.

Questions for Personal Reflection:

- Can you think of where you are finding Jesus as you walk through your own life?

- Does your heart break for something you feel a burden for?

- How can you feed that burden?

- Is there something that causes you to not feed that burden? What are you afraid of?

Fatu's main room before renovations

Fatu's main room after renovations

Before and after of Fatu's bedrooms

Esther before on left: One year later Esther on right

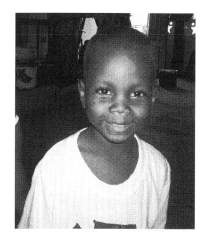

Joshua before on left: One year later Joshua on right

Delivering a whole landrover full of food to Fatu's home

Celebration day for remodeled home. Fatu, Desa'ree, myself & Joshua

Jennifer at Fatu's home

CHAPTER 6

SURVIVAL BY GOD'S GRACE

"For he will deliver the needy who cry out, the afflicted who have no one to help. He will take pity on the weak and the needy and save the needy from death."

– *Psalm 72:12-13*

Fear crippled Sebastion and Fatu Smith as they listened to the rebels coming down the road towards their home once again. The sounds of shooting and yelling followed by screams of terror from victims in their path brought panic to everyone in earshot. They knew this sound all too well after many years of civil war in their country, Liberia. By the year 1995, they had already vacated their home many times, barely escaping with their lives in each instance. With every return, they would come back to a completely destroyed and stripped house, having lost all their possessions.

On this particular day, Sebastion had no strength left to run. In his 60's, he was not in the best of health. These last years of trauma and being on the run had taken a great toll physically as well as emotionally on their whole family, but particularly on him because of his age.

As the rebels came closer and closer, Fatu gathered her younger children and began to run, begging Sebastion to rally the strength to leave with them, just one more time.

He gasped in turmoil and replied that he just could not run anymore. He said, "When they come in this time. I will just let them kill me. I have no more strength left. I just cannot do this again."

Fatu kept yelling for him to come with them. "Please do not give up for the kids' sake and mine! Please do not do this to us. We need you. You just cannot stay here; they will kill you!" She would later recall the sheer panic she felt at the thought of the rebels killing her husband.

As she ran out, she was still screaming for him to come to his senses and leave with them – to no avail. Sebastion, knowing his life would soon be taken, decided he was going to die as a man with dignity. He took a chair, put it on the front porch of his home and sat down. He then draped a towel around his neck, knowing that the rebel groups killed all the men by beheading them. He prepared himself to die as he heard the shouts and gunfire coming closer and closer to him. This is Sebastion Smith's recollection of that time, in his own words:

As I sat on the concrete porch of the front view of our home, the rebels armed with AK-47s and grenades rushed into the compound, shooting everywhere. They were surprised, considering my calmness in the face of impending death. One of them remarked: "I know this old man! He is a former minister in the government. He must die! Before we shoot him, we must first shoot to kill the young people around him." On that note they seized the two boys who were around me. One of them was a former government soldier who was the younger brother of Fatu, and the other was my nephew. "I know you; you're a government soldier," they said to Fatu's brother, "and so we will kill you first."

They told her brother to walk six feet away from them to give him sufficient arm length to shoot at him. With this deadly threat, I immediately jumped to my feet and took these boys close to my chest and told the rebel, "If you want to kill them, you have to kill all of us. So go ahead and shoot." The rebel began to shoot between our legs, but he did not shoot to kill us. In the midst of this pandemonium we saw a Nigerian peacekeeper jeep entering the yard from the same camp whose soldiers my wife was catering to. The rebels jumped into their pick-up and rushed out of the compound. The peacekeeping soldiers told me to explain what was happening. After my explanation, they advised that I should vacate my home and to go to another home in the neighborhood to avoid them coming back for us.

That evening we did just as the peacekeeping soldiers advised. We went to another home in the neighborhood. Early that following morning, two rebels were sent to get me based on the orders of their commander. They found out where I was staying in the neighborhood, and when they arrived, they told me that if I refused to go with them, they would carry my dead body to their commander. I sat calmly and reached the decision not to follow them alive. At this very same moment a peacekeeper truck entered the yard. My wife disembarked from the big truck and came on the scene while the rebels were trying to get me to go with them. When the rebels saw my wife approaching me, and noticed that a peacekeeping truck brought her in, they immediately vacated our presence. My wife, with our seven children, wasted no time to enter the peacekeeping truck, which drove us to a church compound in Garnersville, to safety. Two weeks after our stay at that church compound, it was reported that the Paynesville area was safe again. So I decided to go back to my home for comfort. When my kids and I arrived at our compound, we were only there for about a week when the situation erupted again. We were again forced to leave our home and to run along with thousands of other Liberians to flee the Paynesville area back to the church compound in Garnersville.

Within hours of arriving at the church, gunfire began to be heard outside of the compound, and fear crippled us all once again. My kids' safety was my biggest concern. The next day, a peacekeeping war tank entered the church compound along with four armed peacekeeping soldiers. The war tank commander said to me, "Your wife sent us for you and the kids." Immediately, my entire family and I, including my one-year-old son Patrey, entered the war tank. This was a huge relief, yet still very terrifying.

As the war tank drove through the firing lines of the incoming rebels, the rebels began to fire at the peacekeeping war tank. The peacekeeper soldiers that were in the tank also began to fire back at the rebels, killing a couple of them. In the exchange of gunfire, my one-year-old son Patrey sustained slight wounds on his face from the empty bullets shells discharged from the firing arms of the peacekeeping soldiers inside the war tank. But we were safe from our impending death. From this point, we drove to where my wife Fatu was waiting for us in safety. Fatu was so thankful and relieved to see us alive. She brought us with her to Kakata where she was operating her canteen for the soldiers.

Because Fatu had already gained the trust of many peacekeeping soldiers who she had served at her restaurant, she was hired to run a canteen for the peacekeeping soldiers at each displaced camp they were guarding. They did not hire just anyone for fear that a spy from the rebel group may be among one of the cooks. Their food could easily be poisoned if a cook was actually a spy. This happened in other camps where the men turned up dead after eating a meal. So they exclusively hired Fatu for the position because of their complete trust in her.

After fleeing her home on the day her husband refused to follow, she arrived at the camp in an absolute panic and immediately began to plead with them to help her family. She told them her husband was going to be killed any minute and that they must go save him. She threatened them, saying if they did not try to save her husband, she would not cook for them, and they would be as good as dead because a stranger would probably come from the rebel group and poison them. She scared them by telling them their greatest fears would come to pass if a stranger had to do the cooking. They quickly evaluated the situation and decided they had no choice but to help Fatu for their own safety and well-being. They jumped in their truck and drove down the road and into Sebastion and Fatu's yard. The rebel group left immediately when they saw the peacekeeping truck. This was one of many rescue missions they would make to save Fatu's husband and children. Fatu was overwhelmed with joy each time these men saved her husband and children's lives.

As they were both recanting this story, Sebastion, with tears in his eyes, said "She has saved my life many other times, too. She has definitely been a wonderful wife, one who has never given up on me."

He talked about them traveling from one country to the next during the intense war times. They had no choice at times but to walk for many miles to escape being killed. Sometimes he would just collapse and tell her that he could not go on anymore. It was always Fatu, 23 years his junior, who would figure out how to get him to walk again and not lose hope for living.

Fatu then shared that if it were not for Sebastion taking care of her when she escaped from her abusive Muslim husband, she would not have been able to survive. "God used him to save my life first, and so what I do for him is what any wife would do." Fatu then began to tell me of how God spared her life personally during these scary war times. This is her story, in her own words:

Each time the peacekeeping soldiers would move to an area that was free of rebel activities, they would ask me to go along with them to continue my catering service. They took me to Garnersville, VOA, Careysburg, and Kakata. At the VOA displaced camp, I saw some very terrible things. One day a nice peacekeeping soldier came to my canteen and asked if he could pay for his food and have me keep it for him until he returned from the battle front. Of course I agreed to this. Soon after this agreement, that same young soldier, to my utmost astonishment, was brought from the battlefront with a ruptured stomach, holding on to his intestines with his hands. This was a terrible thing to witness, knowing this man was suffering greatly and would soon die from his wounds.

At one point, a new battalion of peacekeepers came into the area to replace the outgoing battalion. At this same time, the rebels took advantage of this exchange and started firing like crazy on the new peacekeepers, killing most of them. My son Christopher and I found ourselves in the hot firing exchange of gunfire with bullets flying over our heads. My son and I ran hand-in-hand into a building and prostrated ourselves on the floor. After an hour or so the shooting subsided. A peacekeeper ended up rescuing my son and me by putting us into a war tank. We were then taken back to the city of Monrovia where our home was. This was a very terrifying thing for my son and me to experience.

When the VOA displaced camp was cleared from the rebel's command, the peacekeepers moved to Kakata to clear the rebels there. After Kakata was completely cleared by the mutual peace agreement, the peacekeepers brought me to Kakata to re-establish my canteen. Occasionally it became necessary for me to commute between Monrovia and Kakata to purchase food and drinks for the canteen. At that time I was strictly advised not to travel in any commercial vehicles due to the danger level in this. So each time the peacekeepers were traveling to Monrovia to do shopping, I would go along with them to purchase food and drinks. I would also visit my home where my husband and children were. It was necessary for me to leave them with food money for their survival.

On one of these fateful days, the peacekeepers dropped me off at Red Light (a busy shopping area outside of Monrovia). I bought my food and put it down at a shop known by the peacekeepers. I then rushed to Paynesville to my family to leave food money for them. By the time I got back to Red Light, I found out that the peacekeepers had been blowing the car horn for me at the shop, but I was not around. They decided to take my goods with them back to

Kakata for me, not knowing where I was. At this point I was forced to hire a commercial vehicle to get back to Kakata. This was a very risky decision because the peacekeepers had warned me to never do this. The taxi that I hired started out from Monrovia with two occupants. As we drove on, we picked up one peacekeeper on the Kakata highway at Todee junction. It was a relief to me to take along an armed man. The man who had been sitting in the front gave up his seat to this peacekeeper and came and sat back with me. As we drove on and got close to Morrison Farm, we fell into an ambush as we ascended the hill. We suddenly saw a rebel, half-naked, standing in the middle of the road with a gun pointing at our vehicle.

I shouted at the driver and told him that it was a rebel and to not stop. I was yelling at him to keep moving. The driver listened to me and kept driving straight toward the rebel without slowing down. The rebel jumped out of the road to avoid being hit by our vehicle. As he did this, firing began to come from all sides targeting our vehicle. As all four tires were deflated, I knew we were in serious trouble. Running on the iron rings of the vehicle, the nervous driver was terrified and wanted to stop. I kept yelling at the driver to not stop but to keep going. During this time, I hung my head down between the driver's seat and the peacekeeper's seat up front. I soon realized that a bullet had hit the man sitting beside me through the back of his head. He quickly collapsed onto me with his head lying on my shoulder and his eyes wide open, completely dead. This was a terrible and scary sight. All the bullets had come from the back because we had been passing the ambush spot.

I then noticed one of the bullets had also pierced through the back of the peacekeeper's seat, entering his stomach through his back. Iron particles from the seat were bursting out of his stomach with a heavy pool of blood flowing everywhere. Our vehicle came to an abrupt halt at a place where the peacekeepers could hear all the firing on our vehicle. They quickly began to render assistance to our vehicle. As they opened our damaged vehicle door, they noticed that there were only two survivors: the driver and myself. I saw a horrible sight when the peacekeeper was holding his bloody stomach, saying his last words to his commander, " O ga, I don dia for Liberia o." This is a statement said in Liberian English by men who, with their last breath in battle, would declare that their death was for Liberia. My entire body was drenched in blood, but not a scratch was on my body. To God be the Glory! He had saved my life again for a purpose.

Over the years, I have truly grown to love the Smiths; they are an amazing couple. Recently Sebastion had a stroke and is pretty much confined to his bedroom, yet his mind is as strong as ever. We often talk about God's faithfulness and amazing intervention in all of our lives. Sebastion is currently working on writing his and Fatu's life story in detail. After his stroke, he can no longer write with his right hand, but he has taught himself to write with his left hand beautifully. He is highly educated and has two master's degrees from universities in the United States.

Looking back, it is hard to believe that this is a couple who could not feed their children for three days when we first met them. This is a couple who has been so faithful, trying to raise 80 kids, as a loving mom and dad with nothing to gain personally. This is a couple who has shown integrity in all they are doing for their family and community, and they love God with all their hearts. They are both pastors and are reaching out to help all those in their path. This is a couple who no one would help because their home was in an uncertified category due to its terrible conditions.

This couple is who we met, and who God prompted us to help, and now they are living a life with a future. They have a home with their many children who now have sanitary conditions. Fatu has also started three business endeavors to help secure an income on their own. They are working hard to become self-sustained.

This couple was in poverty due to some very terrible circumstances, yet they have proven so eager to help themselves. We did not come in with long-term sponsorship in mind; we came in with relief first and then, through relationship, put a plan of action together to figure out how we could be a part of the solution to enable them to help themselves. Without this initial act of mercy, we would not have gotten to know these inspiring people.

Through our relationship with them:

- Our hearts have been forever changed.

- Our faith and love for God has developed.

- Our love and compassion for those in poverty have grown.

- Our eyes have been opened to the fact that everyone in poverty has a story and desires dignity.

- We have learned that dignity can be restored through love, value and relationship.

- We acquired a love for all the hurting Liberian children and orphanage directors who were in desperate need of intervention for their sheer survival.

Questions for Personal Reflection:

- Are you prepared to go out of your comfort zone and build friendships with those who are suffering to find out what their story is without judgment?

- Are you willing to be a part of their solution if they are willing to help themselves as you help them?

SERVING IS RARELY GLAMOROUS

The Lord is near to the brokenhearted and saves the crushed in spirit.

– Psalms 34:18

The tumor on the 15-year-old boy's face was large and already out of control. "It is inoperable," said the doctor on the big white ship. "There is nothing we can do for him. You must take him home and make him comfortable in these last days of his life." The parents of George Sumo Jr. were devastated at this news. Their hope to save their oldest son's life was doused by the doctor's words.

They went home to their little one-room rented structure with enormous grief and heavy hearts. A few women from the ship began to visit George Jr. regularly as he became weaker and weaker. They were so grieved for this family. Another thing that was very upsetting to them was the dilapidated tin shack in which the family of seven lived. Everyone in the family slept on one mattress on the floor and had no sanitary facilities anywhere around them. The women from the ship visited George Jr. and performed some hospice care to make him more comfortable. It was not too long after that he painfully slipped away from this life.

When he died, these women were determined not to forget this family. George Sr. did not have a job, so they got him a day job on the ship. They found out that his wife was willed a little piece of property when her parents died, so they put a plan together to raise money to build a home for the family. One of the women came to my husband, who was working in the renovations department, and asked if he would oversee the project if they raised all the money for it.

They had found out that we had already started an orphanage project off the ship, and they pleaded with Tim to consider taking on this building project too. Since it was just a few other co-workers and me who were leaving the ship daily to work on the orphanage project, Tim came to me with this proposed idea.

I immediately said absolutely not, as I had a very full plate already with the other project. All my personal focus was for that home. I just didn't think it would be wise to spread ourselves too thin. My husband, however, did not take that answer as a definite no and invited George Sr. into our cabin to meet me. I was a little distressed over this because I knew he was already grieving from his son's death, and I did not want to be the one to tell him that we could not help him. I had no intention of taking that project on.

When I met George Sr. he was a thin, sad man. He had a precious spirit and was very kind as he told me about his dream to have a home for his family. I listened, though my mind was already made up, and told George Sr. that at that time we could not do anything for him. What I could do, though, was give him some food for his family. So I went down three flights of stairs, climbed the ladder down to the large cargo hold in our renovations department and manually brought up numerous bags of food up the ladder one by one. I was dripping with sweat when I got back to George

Sr. bringing with me a man I recruited in the hall to help me carry the food. George Sr., of course, was so grateful, and I was happy that I could at least send him home with something to help feed his family.

The galley crew on the ship, along with a very determined young man named Matthew Cramer, took it upon themselves to raise all the money for George Sr.'s house, even without knowing who would take on the task of building it. Once they had most of the money raised, they came to us again, requesting that we take this on. With hesitation, Matt Le Page, our dedicated foreman on Fatu's project, and I agreed, since most of the money had already been raised and they didn't have anyone else to oversee the project. We had no idea what we were really getting into, but we did finally say yes.

Tim and Matt Le Page went to George Sr.'s property to work out the initial plans of the home. To their surprise, the property was located way behind the busiest market area in all of Liberia. To get to his property, they had to drive through the center of this huge market, treacherously dodging people who were shopping in the crazy area called "Red Light." They literally had to drive at a snail's pace, honking continuously as they moved forward through the sea of people and hoping those in front of their vehicle would part so they could get through. This made everything about the job very complicated and difficult – especially delivering supplies.

For the next six weeks, Matt and I and our Liberian co-worker Morris would come to know that route very well. It never got any easier getting in and out of that place, but we definitely learned how to maneuver our Land Rovers and use our horns a lot.

George Sr.'s house took about five weeks to finish, and we were so grateful when it was finally done. It took more energy than we had expected to oversee the locals working on this. So it was with a big sigh of relief that we moved George Sr.'s family into their new home. It was truly a great celebration.

When I was taking George Sr. to work on the ship one day, he began to tell me the whole story of how difficult it was to raise his children in the small shack in which they had lived. I was tired and did not have a very good attitude. I had done plenty of running around that day, and everything had seemed to go wrong. Because of my tiredness, I intended to stay silent while George Sr. was in the car.

He, on the other hand, was quite talkative. He told me how he had been dreaming and praying for over ten years to have a home for his family. He had not been able to work for many years because of the war. Then his son got sick, and it consumed most of their time, energy and money to care for him until his death. So there in the car, with tears in his eyes, he poured out his heart of gratitude. He thanked me and shared how grateful he was for all those who gave towards his home.

As George Sr. was sharing, God unexpectedly broke my heart for this man in such a deep way. I was silently moved to tears. I had sunglasses on, so George Sr. did not see the tears dripping from my eyes, but his life story broke my heart. I got a huge glimpse of God's heart for George Sr. and his family in such a tangible way that afternoon.

Furthermore, I started to feel so convicted about my attitude toward this project. In all the hardship of getting this home done, it had been difficult to stay positive. Yet from that day forward I no longer looked at this as a burden but felt it was a privilege. **I am learning that most miracles happen through our inconveniences.** We just need to be willing to be inconvenienced in order to facilitate what God wants to accomplish. Mother Teresa stated this very well in one of her quotes: ***"Love, to be real, it must cost—it must*** *hurt—it must empty us of self.* I have learned this to be a true statement over and over again in numerous circumstances.

Each time we see George Sr. he runs over to us and gives us the biggest, longest hugs. He still hunts us down when we come to Liberia to show his gratitude once again. He will always have a special place our hearts.

There were others who were instrumental in raising the finances that made sure George Sr. and his family were set up when they moved in. Matthew Cramer, our Mercy Ships galley friends and numerous others came alongside us to make this project successful. They were all critical in making his house a functional and healthy place for his family.

While doing this project on the side, so to speak, we had to find a cook to feed our hired Liberian workers. In Liberia, it is customary to feed your employees daily. When we drove up to the cook's home, I noticed a little girl who was about seven years old lying on a mat on the ground outside the home, looking very sick.

I walked up to her, felt her little forehead and noticed she had a very high fever. I asked her mother what was wrong with her, and she said the child had malaria. Most people who feel sick in Liberia will tell you that they have malaria; it is kind of like us in America saying we have the flu when we don't feel well, yet as I looked at this girl, I knew her life was in danger. She was in great distress and very, very sick. There was a clinic within walking distance of this woman's home, so I told the mother that she needed to take her daughter to the doctor. She informed me that she could not do that because her husband would not approve. She said her husband was Muslim and against her going to the clinic. If she took her child, she would be in a whole lot of trouble from him. Hearing this I was appalled. Was she really willing to let her daughter die for fear of what her husband might do? What about her child's life?

I had my Liberian friend and co-worker with me and asked him what to do. He advised me that this was simply the Muslim culture here and it would be best not to cross them. It is not like in America when we go against our husband's wishes; the consequences are very severe for these women if they cross their Muslim spouses. I was so angry! I continued to plead with the mother to take the child to the clinic, with no success. I looked at the little girl and sat down beside her in great distress. I found out her name and then laid my hands on her and said a prayer. "Oh Lord, will you please heal little Teresa and spare her life? You are this little girl's only hope in this very desperate situation. All I can do is to leave her in your hands now."

Even after my prayer, I was so tempted to just defy the mother's orders and take Teresa to a clinic. I knew that if she did have malaria, it was treatable with a simple oral medication readily available at every clinic. But inside I felt like God gave me a strong warning not to do that.

So I left this little girl in God's hands, knowing there was nothing more I could do, and walked away. This was a very deep internal struggle for me. I continued to pray for little Teresa over the next couple of days.

When we returned a few days later, to my absolute excitement, Teresa ran up to my car, eager to see me. I was thrilled – she looked completely well. We hung out while I was checking out the house being built next door for George Sr. She had so much energy, running around catching frogs in the swamp to roast and eat. Once roasted, she kept trying to share her little skinny frog with me. I was a bit grossed out, and I very politely kept turning her down, saying frogs were not something I really wanted to try. This then became a silly game for her, as she loved getting a reaction out of me.

When she was done eating her frog, she came up behind me as I was sitting in a chair and began stroking my hair.

Her hands were very dirty, but I didn't care. Tears welled up in my eyes with gratefulness for this sweet life. I was just so happy she was alive. This precious girl stole my heart that day.

My heart was so full with gratitude to God for answering my prayers for Teresa. God truly touched and completely healed her sick little body. That day, God showed me that, in spite of man's mistakes, we have the power to change the outcome of so much through our prayers. In my helplessness, prayer unlocked God's perfect will for Teresa's life. There have been numerous times since that day that God has brought healing and intervention in some very helpless situations as we have prayed.

Just imagine what could happen if we all chose to live each day beyond ourselves, with the sheer touch of God spilling out of us onto each person in our path. Our selfish lives would be transformed and we would realize that we were actually meant to live this kind of life for the sake of seeing others set free. God is so ready for this. Are we?

Questions for Personal Reflection:

- Are you willing to be available for whatever God may ask of you?

- Is anything hindering you from being available?

- Is your negative attitude about something or someone causing you not to be blessed in a certain area of your life?

Matt LePage and the building crew at George Sr's house

George Sr.'s family

George Sr.'s house towards the end of construction

*Matthew Cramer and crew making sure the inside
was ready for George Sr.'s family*

This was our daily drive through the market to George Sr.'s home.

~~~~~~~~~~~~~~~~~~~

Chapter 8

REMEMBERING THE DREAM

~~~~~~~~~~~~~~~~~~~

"You may not be able to describe it. You may have forgotten it. You may even no longer believe in it. But it's there."

– Bruce Wilkerson

"Becky, please stay away from the dangerous water," scolded my mother each time I wandered from her side. Walking along the dangerous, yet beautiful seashore of Manzanillo, Mexico, was a great fear for every mother in the area.

My father was preaching at a local church that night, and my mother had four restless young children who she needed to keep occupied through his sermon. A local young woman named Maria, who was seven months pregnant and very uncomfortable, coaxed my mother into taking a walk on the beach with her near the church. She assured my mother, who was also seven months pregnant, that she would help her walk with all of us children.

My mother, eager to get us all some fresh air, gladly agreed to the walk. Signs were posted at the beach not to touch the very dangerous shorelines because of the strong undercurrents. Maria reinforced the warning by telling us all to keep very close to her and my mom. She told some stories of her ventures as a marathon swimmer and talked about respecting the ocean's extreme currents in this particular area, where it was possible for someone to be pulled out to sea within seconds.

Being almost five years old, I didn't know the implications of not listening to her strict warnings. My one and only concern at that time was keeping my brand new sandals from flipping off my feet as I walked through the sand. I remember having to keep stopping to adjust my shoe regularly, as they would flip off with the weight of the sand running through them.

The next memory I have of that day was my sandal flipping off my foot. When I reached down to retrieve it, I lost all balance to stand. Without knowing how, I ended up in the water and was suddenly spinning underneath the surface, tunneling out to sea.

My mother immediately went into a panic, and Maria knew she had to do something. It basically takes only two waves to take you completely out to sea, where you can be lost forever. With no time to waste, Maria immediately risked her life and ran out to save me, with only seconds to spare before the next wave came. I remember her collapsing with me on the shore, completely exhausted, as I began to cry hysterically – partly in shock and partly because I had lost my new sandals. I wouldn't know until years later just how close I was to death that evening on the beach.

My distant memory of this trauma was rolling underwater over and over, pounding against the sand and trying to figure out which way was up. I was completely disoriented and desperate to find air. I would have nightmares of this out-of-control feeling for years to come. Still to this day, I have a very healthy fear of strong currents.

My mother recounted this story often, talking about how God spared my life through Maria, who risked both herself and her unborn child to save me. "The angels were working overtime," she used to say. When I talked to my father about this incident recently, he brought up the symbolism that **God used a young pregnant, Mexican woman, living in poverty, to save my life, and now God is using my life to save children who are living in the same conditions of poverty that Maria lived in**. My dad's friend, named Sandy, leaned over as my dad was talking and said "Oh, I bet God is looking down and smiling at all of this!" Tears came to my eyes as I got a glimpse of God's heart in that moment. Something that happened so many years ago paralleled my life now.

What a story of grace. A life rescued, and a woman who risked everything. She had no idea that her heroic actions would affect thousands of lives in the future. I was oblivious to any of this, and yet **God was weaving and spinning many things to accomplish His perfect will in my life, for the purpose of bringing His will to pass in others' lives**.

Looking back to see the grace and protection that God has had in my life is a humbling thing. It is also amazing to see that we are products of how we grew up. Either bad or good, our past does play a role in our future. I am so thankful that God covers the negative parts of our upbringing if we will allow Him to. At the same time, He teaches us how to embrace the positive things and carry them into the future. As it says in Romans 8:28, God truly does bring all things to work out for good to those who love Him.

Being raised as a missionary kid until I was eight definitely made for an adventurous life. My parents were missionaries in Mexico until we moved up to Washington state to be close to my dad's aging father.

As kids, we had no idea of the hardships my parents went through during those years in Mexico. We just knew they had an incredible love for God, us and those whom they came to serve. Evangelistic services were a focal point of their ministry, sharing about the redemptive power of a personal relationship with Jesus, but they were also feeding children in the garbage dumps and aiding those in need wherever humanly possible.

All five of us kids became tenderized and forever broken for those in extreme poverty, both physically and spiritually. To this day, we all have a real heart for those who are hurting, in part because of what we were exposed to in our younger years.

We never had much, yet my parents taught us not to look the other way when we saw the desperate needs of others. There were many times when we could not do anything to physically help people in need, but if there was opportunity, then we always saw my parents taking extra moments to bless those in their path, even if it was just with a simple prayer.

People were never looked down upon for their race, religion or financial status. Everyone was an equal in my parents' eyes. I am so grateful for their example. They left a legacy for us to follow in showing worth and value to all human beings.

Another thing that plays a large role in our lives as we grow up is our childhood dreams. I love the book *The Dream Giver* by David Wilkinson. It talks about God giving each of us a dream from the time we were young. He writes, "You may not be able to describe it. You may have forgotten it. You may even no longer believe in it. But it's there."

Wilkinson talks about these dreams sometimes taking years before they are fulfilled, and about how sometimes they are actually never fulfilled, all according to the choices we make in our lifetime. God knew us intimately before we were ever born. He created our innermost being and knows what will bring ultimate fulfillment through Him as we use our gifts and talents for His glory here on Earth (*Psalm 139:13*). There are specific things He has for us to do on Earth according to what He has birthed deep within us from the beginning.

Indeed, God did birth a big dream in me when I was young, yet it took many years for me to actually remember that this dream even existed. After I read Bruce's book, I began to ask God "What was my childhood dream?" A few dreams were easy for me to remember because I was living out those dreams (to be a wife and mom). Yet, I knew there was probably another dream that I wasn't remembering. After weeks of pondering, the dream that I had long forgotten came back into my memory.

As a young child, I recalled watching a "Feed the Hungry" commercial on TV and just sobbing and sobbing as I watched images of starving little children on the screen. My father walked into the room and saw me crying. When he noticed what I was watching, he quickly went to the TV and turned it off. He said, "Becky, that stuff is too difficult to handle when you are so young. It is best not to watch those images right now." He clearly did not want me to be upset. When the TV went off, I remember making an internal promise to myself that someday I would help starving and hungry children. My thought was that no child should ever go hungry and suffer for lack of food.

It wasn't until I was in Africa years later that this dream came to be a reality and its memory was relived in a very powerful way. It has been very interesting and amazing to walk in a sphere that God has specifically ordained for me to walk in — one that was dormant for so many years. As I walk forward in this newfound dream, I have had a whole new level of fulfillment in partnership with God that I could not have dreamed of before.

In making this statement, I also want to say that it is so critical to pay attention to God's timing when we set out to make our dreams a reality. It is extremely important to make sure we are not going ahead of God's schedule. In His timing, we have His blessing, favor and power with us. If we try to push something through on our own without consulting God, we will be walking down a very difficult and painful road. And that is when burnout, exhaustion and/ or family destruction are imminent. If I had begun to live out my dream as a young mother, my kids and family would have been harmed. God made it so clear when the kids were young that they had to have my full and undivided focus. Yes, I was still involved in ministry, but I had to be involved minimally to ensure our kids were being raised in a healthy manner.

Even now, what I am privileged to be a part of comes with a great responsibility. With fear and trembling, I must always make sure that my husband, kids and home are always the first priority. This is God's number one calling for my life from the moment I committed to be Tim's wife, saying "I do" on our wedding day.

My kids, Brianna, Desa'ree and Joshua, are the greatest, most treasured gifts that God has entrusted to Tim and I. I do not want to get to Heaven and hear God say, "Great job with all those needy orphans you helped. Yet in the process of helping all those children, you made your own children orphans by not being there for them. Therefore you neglected my heart for your biological children to be raised healthy and whole." This would be a terrible tragedy.

God has worked hard to help me understand this. Sometimes it comes through correction, sometimes through having others cross our path who were emotionally destroyed from parents who went out to fulfill their own dreams, leaving their kids to figure out how to grow up on their own. The number of hurting children and young adults who went through our mission programs was a stark reminder of kids having parents living with them who were completely absent emotionally from their children. These parents were too involved in their own issues and trying to fulfill their own dreams. This made me wary of being the cause of my kids' destruction.

One of these lessons came in the form of correction from the Lord. Before we worked in Africa, my husband and I led high school summer programs with outreaches to Mexico for approximately six years while we were working with Mercy Ships in Texas. Our goal was to introduce the kids to an adventurous and loving God while giving them the opportunity to serve the poor and needy in a foreign place.

One summer we worked at an orphanage where there were only children up to the age of two in the home. Each of these children was fully adoptable and so precious. On one of the visits Tim was the highlight of the kids' afternoon (which is no surprise to anyone who knows my husband). He was playing with a handful of kids and having a ball. They were literally wrapped all around my 6'5 husband. He was a total jungle gym for them. They were so cute, talking to Tim a mile a minute in Spanish. He did not understand what they were saying, but the language of love seems to have no barriers with this age group. They were giggling and singing and just having a sweet time.

When it came time to leave, they suddenly became traumatized that their new jungle gym was going to leave. They clung to him so tightly and began to cry. The workers came over and tried to peel them off of Tim. This became a time-consuming process due to the sheer wills of these little ones. Once loosed from Tim, they were literally screaming, holding out their little arms to my husband, begging him not to leave them. Oh, how our emotions went wild with those images, as we had to walk away! This deeply affected us, especially my husband. Images like those are not easily forgotten.

When we went back to the United States, I could not get these kids out of my mind. Many friends would ask me regularly to keep my eyes open for a child who they could possibly adopt from one the homes where we volunteered.

After this particular summer, I had a huge burden to make this a reality for my friends. I checked with that particular orphanage home and found out that all the adoption forms could be picked up for free at their office. They would not charge me anything on their side if I did all the work myself. I took this as a door that was wide open from God. I put a whole plan of action together on the American side as well as on the Mexican side. I researched everything well. I would open a non-profit adoption agency to make this all work. This was a fool-proof plan that I felt could not go wrong.

I figured out that this orphanage in Mexico would be the least expensive for my friends, and I decided I would donate my services (minus my expenses) in order to help these couples adopt children. I also formulated a plan for the following summer to have all our teams' volunteer efforts centered around this particular home so we could get to know all the kids, as well as the staff, for future implementation of my idea. At that time, my own kids were eight, 10 and 13. My life was full, actually too full, but my heart was overflowing with this great idea, and I knew this would help so many. Somehow this would all work out.

As the summer approached, my excitement was absolutely uncontainable. I could not wait to get to Mexico and go forward with all this.

As we approached the border of Mexico with two busloads of 80+ staff and junior high and high school kids, my logistical duties kicked into full gear. It was time to get these teams over the border smoothly. These crossings were usually hours and hours, so it was never an easy scenario. It involved changing buses from stateside to Mexico, as well as bag checks and paperwork.

This particular time it seemed like everything went wrong. Border guards wanted bribes, kids were crying thinking they were not going to get in the country, and staff members had misplaced various pieces of paperwork. It was one of those nightmare crossings. Finally, 10 hours later, we were let through.

By 2 a.m., we arrived in Monterrey, Mexico, and all I could think of was getting into a bed. Oh, did that bed feel good – even with stifling hot temperatures and no air conditioning. I was completely exhausted, yet I was also excited for what this trip was going to symbolize with the new adoption venture coming up.

As morning arrived, I woke up with the most excruciating headache. I literally could not move because I was in so much pain. It had been almost 10 years since I had suffered a migraine headache as bad as this one. It was completely debilitating.

Tim and the team, as well as my own kids, awoke with excitement for the day, as I just lay there, unable to function. To my horror, I realized I would be spending the day in bed while they all went on their way to their specific places of ministry.

On day number two, my body continued to feel horrible. I literally could not peel myself off the bed. My head still hurt terribly. By this time I was so frustrated and upset. I was completely bound to my bed. I knew precious days were slipping away, and this was not what I needed to happen to my body. I had things to do, places to go and people to meet.

By that time I had started asking God some pointed questions. I needed some answers – now. "Oh God, why haven't you healed my body yet? I have a job to do for all my friends who are expecting me to find their babies here. Why, why, why?"

As I was begging through my tears, asking God to speak something, I got a very clear and direct answer from Him in my heart. It was an answer that I totally did not expect to get. This is what He began to speak to my heart: "*This new adventure and plan is not in my timing; you never asked me about this. You just assumed this was me. This is your adventure, and it will take all your time and energy and destroy your family. Your number one priority is your husband, and his ministry, as well as to make sure your kids are raised into healthy children who love me with all their hearts."* I felt like God asked me very clearly to lay the dream down and never pick up something like this again unless it was clearly His plan and timing. I also felt like He told me not to even step foot in that particular orphanage home again unless it was actually Him asking me to go into it.

There was much internal trauma and despair that came from that realization. I could not believe what God was asking me to do. After all the preparation, this was extremely painful.

As I lay there too sick and miserable to do anything, I cried for mercy from the Lord. "Oh God, I am so sorry." As I thought more about it through the day, it dawned on me that I just assumed God would be into this. It was going to be such a great thing for so many. I didn't take into consideration that God may not be pleased with me doing this. I was completely shocked. My heart hurt over this revelation. My pride also took a huge beating.

After many tears and many conversations with God, I made a commitment that I would not take on anything of significance from that point forward without having God's complete direction and what I call "handprints" all over it. I would not waste my time any more on things I thought were good. From that day forward, I would only go for the best of God's highest plan for my life.

I love how Oswald Chambers states it in one of his devotionals – *"**The Good is always the enemy of the Best.**" God has the best in mind for us, yet we tend to settle for the good.*

All the time I had wasted putting together this adoption stuff really began to grieve my heart, especially knowing

God was not in what I was doing. I am very determined, and when I set my mind on something, I am an all or nothing person. So, in looking back now, I know that God was so right. At that time in my life, my family truly would have suffered. God had to teach me quite a bit more in life before He could entrust me with bigger things.

My kids are now 21, 18 and 16 and very independent. They still need their mom around though. They still need my strong presence in their lives emotionally. This is part of healthy living. As God has released more in the area of ministry, I continue to take my first responsibility very seriously.

If we are not faithful with the ordinary tasks of life, God cannot entrust us with bigger things.

If we push ourselves to have big things on our plates, yet have not learned to be faithful with the small, ordinary tasks in life, then those big tasks will not be accomplished well. They will eventually fall apart and cause pain to those around us. In observing people's lives, I've seen that those who have learned faithfulness and diligence with the things they may feel are insignificant prove to be very faithful when entrusted with bigger things. Faithfulness and diligence are keys to seeing amazing results from our lives.

Being faithful as a mom and wife, making sure my kids have food to eat, a clean house to live in and a mom who is there for them emotionally is actually just as important as saving orphans halfway across the world. My first duty is to this family that God has entrusted to me. If I am not faithful with that role, how can I expect to see amazing results in the orphanage work or anything else I am privileged to do?

Faithfulness always needs to start with what is in front of me. Learning this lesson teaches me how to be faithful in every other aspect of my life.

It has also been critical for our kids not to grow up resenting our involvement with helping others. They have Tim's and my full attention, yet they are also asked to open their eyes wide to the needs around them. My prayer is that they will learn by example on this one.

Matthew 25:23 (NIV) *"Well done, good and faithful servant! You have been faithful with a few things; I will put you in charge of many things. Come and share your master's happiness!"*

Questions for Personal Reflection:

- What is your childhood dream?

- Are you living that dream? If not, what steps could you take to make it a reality?

- Is there something you are pursuing that may not be God's will for this time in your life?

- What are some things that you may be wasting your time on that you think are good but may not be God's best?

CHAPTER 9

DEPRESSION TO EXPRESSION

> *"Accepting the reality of our broken, flawed lives is the beginning of spirituality not because the spiritual life will remove our flaws but because we let go of seeking perfection and, instead, seek God, the one who is present in the tangledness of our lives."*
>
> – Michael Yaconelli

Depressed? How could I be depressed? I didn't feel sad. These were the thoughts running through my mind one night, as Tim and I were in different rooms watching the same television show. A pharmaceutical commercial came on, and the spokeswoman was asking these questions. "Are you an insomniac, wanting to sleep all day? Do you have difficulty making normal daily decisions? Do you lack motivation to do any normal tasks in life? If you said yes to these things, then you may be clinically depressed. Ask your doctor about this medication that may help you," she said. Tim yelled from the other room, "Oh my gosh, honey! That is what you have. You're depressed! You need help!"

That was the first time it even somewhat crossed my mind that I really may not be well mentally and emotionally. I had just thought I was exhausted from all the circumstances I had just walked through. I justified lying in bed all day every day for days, which then turned into weeks and months.

After the first few years of working full-time in ministry and taking care of three kids with my husband, I didn't bargain on having to deal with a lot of what was thrown my way. I thought coming into full-time ministry with our young family would be an amazing experience. What I did not count on, though, was that my role really wasn't going to change much after leaving our hometown. I had three, four and seven-year-old children, and my full-time job was still going to be working as a mom. The ministry was something Tim could be involved with in those first few years full-time, but my participation was very limited due to the needs of the kids. Our location was different, but my duties as a wife and mom remained the same. I love our kids deeply and love to be with them, but my expectations of serving as a family in ministry really had to be crushed. My ministry involvement was strictly part-time administration for programs that Tim led. I was very much behind the scenes.

I came to the realization that helping to fill Tim's huge need to be in ministry was more important than trying to find something to fulfill *me* in ministry at this season of my life. My focus had to be on the family in order for our kids and marriage to be healthy. I made the choice daily to be a faithful wife and mom and make sure the family was a priority. Laying down my personal agenda and letting God rule my life and circumstances was not an easy thing to do. Looking around me, I realized that many other young mothers who came to work alongside us also had this same expectation. They too had to walk through this disillusionment of what they thought ministry was supposed to be like. This was not easy for any of them either. Laying down these expectations was a key thing I learned at the very beginning of our full-time service in ministry.

As a wife, I loved to see Tim so fulfilled in what he was doing. He was working hard to mentor and train many young adults who came through our programs. It was absolutely amazing to be a part of radically changed lives. Seeing these changed lives are what kept things so worth all the sacrifice in those early years, and Tim was truly in his element.

As the years passed, Tim and I had regular evaluation moments, asking God if it was time for us to go back to normal jobs. Each time, we would both sense that it was not time to leave yet.

One of these extremely tough times was during a trip to Nicaragua in 2000 when Tim got dengue fever and almost died. He was in bed for over 40 days with extreme pain and very scary symptoms. As his sole caretaker, I had no idea how draining it would be to take care of someone so sick. You will read more of this story in a future chapter of this book.

That following summer my mother became extremely sick, so I also took care of her immediately following Tim's sickness. (She too almost died that summer.) Tim was fully engaged in leading the summer programs with Mercy Ships in Texas, so I kept all three kids right alongside me while I cared for my mom in the Seattle area. Juggling sick loved ones and motherhood was a marathon I do not ever want to repeat. Mentally, these were some of the most draining times of my life.

It was after both Tim and my mother recovered and I was back to home life that this bout of depression came on. The diagnosis for me was one I never thought I would have to personally go through. Yet I saw that I had all the symptoms. I couldn't make any daily decisions such as what to make for dinner, what needed to be done around the house, etc. I had insomnia, only wanting to sleep all day, with no motivation to do anything. I thought my body was just exhausted until others began to give me the depression diagnosis.

It took me a bit of time to finally admit that I was clinically depressed because I didn't feel sad, which is what I thought constituted depression. I did have all the other symptoms, so I finally admitted I needed professional help to get back to emotional normalcy. I knew that without help I was not headed down a good road.

Growing up, my family became very aware of what untreated and unacknowledged depression could do. My younger brother went into full-blown schizophrenia at the age of 16 due to untreated depression. He went from being totally normal and social to completely schizophrenic over a four-month time frame. My brother's doctors said that if our family had been knowledgeable of the signs of depression and known how to help in the beginning stages, he could have been treated for severe depression and had a chance to recover. But we had no idea what any of that was in the 1980s. To this day, he has not recovered and has to be in a mental hospital because of his violent and destructive behavior. This has been a very difficult tragedy for our family. A whole other book could be written about all the things our family has gone through to try to bring him into recovery. We are still praying for that miracle to happen.

Not wanting to go down a similar road as my brother, off to the doctor's office I went. I was put on sleeping pills for a month to get me back on a normal sleeping schedule, and I started exercising daily and forcing myself back into different social settings. The doctor said if I didn't show significant signs of recovery, then she would put me on antidepressants. I worked very hard to push myself to get well.

The social settings were the most difficult things to get back into. My heart would begin to palpitate extremely fast as soon as I encountered a group of people. The anxiety would sometimes be unbearable. Sometimes I would go in the bathroom and just try to breathe calmly and relax; I feared if I didn't, I would pass out. After regaining some control, I would enter the group again. I could not figure out why this happened. It was all crazy. But I persevered and eventually, changes started to happen. I noticed a big difference when I began to sleep fully through the night, and I also saw that the exercise seemed to be helping. My body and mind began to feel stronger.

I completely stepped out of ministry for about a year during this time in order to focus on getting well. Paying attention to my own body and mind so that I could fully recover had to become my top priority. I realized that, through taking care of everyone else, I had not paid attention to my own needs for staying healthy. I was lost in service to others. It was time to start taking care of me. I understood this was not a selfish thing but was necessary and valuable. If I could not take time for myself, I could not be there for my kids and family or anyone else. I started treating myself to things that I had stopped doing years prior, things that would refresh me.

I allowed myself to take long baths in the evenings again. I implemented a walk with God each day, even if it was just a short one. I made my chicken noodle soup from scratch even though no other family member liked it but me. I decided to get my hair done by a professional instead cutting it myself to save money. Date nights with my husband resumed after many years. It amazed me how these very simple things brought me such refreshment. I always had to talk to myself and tell myself I was not selfish for taking care of myself; this was health. The time spent on these simple things was for my own health because it actually made me a happier person.

I never had to take antidepressants, but I continued to keep myself accountable to my doctor. The depression lifted within about three months. The anxiety took almost two years to get over though – it was a remnant of the depression. My doctor said everybody reacts differently to depression, and the first step to recovery is acknowledging that you are sick so you can get help or at least take proactive measures to help yourself.

In my search for answers about my anxiety, I realized that I had perfectionistic tendencies. I unintentionally felt I had to be perfect in every situation. I had to literally speak to myself when I would enter a group of people and say, "You do not have to be perfect. Just be you. Relax. Relax. Relax." Even to this day, if this anxiety starts to rise up, I speak to myself over and over before walking into whatever group I am feeling anxious about, repeating those very same words to myself.

God revealed a lot to me through this time. I became very passionate about putting extra priority on my relationship with God. I needed God to penetrate the depth of my heart and soul in a fresh new way like never before. I began to read the Bible and other Christian books in a more focused way. I was so desperate and hungry for God's presence.

Being caretaker, mom and wife, I realized that I had unintentionally neglected my spiritual life, as well as my physical well-being through the craziness of life. I know many young mothers, as well as those in full-time ministry or service to others, can also relate to this. I was still talking to God and still felt His presence in my life, but I wasn't in a passionate pursuit for more of God daily. I was in survival mode, which soon turned into not surviving at all.

As I started making healthy decisions physically, I also had huge breakthroughs spiritually. A big turning point came when I read a book called *Intercessory Prayer* by Dutch Sheets. This book was challenging and talked about living an amazing life in partnership with God. It sparked the beginning of a whole new empowered life. Dutch wrote about there being no boundaries of what God can do through us as we say "yes" in obedience to whatever He asks us to do.

He talked about why God needs our prayers and partnership and about learning to listen to promptings from the Holy Spirit. **And he explained how our prayers are the keys to unlock the many chains that bind people up.**

I was especially interested in the part where he shared about God needing our partnership to make His kingdom come and His will be done on Earth. He gave scripture after scripture which all confirmed exactly what he was writing about.

One illustration was about Daniel in the Bible reading the prophet Jeremiah's writings. He discovered that it was prophesied that the Israelites' captivity would only last for 70 years. It had almost been 70 years. Instead of just expecting God to set the Israelites free, Daniel suddenly feels the urgency to pray and fast for this to come to pass (Daniel 9:3). Somehow, he understood that prayer had a huge part to play in bringing that prophecy into existence. In Daniel 10:12-13 an angel appeared to Daniel and spoke these words to him: "Do not be afraid, Daniel, for from the first day that you set your heart on understanding this and on humbling yourself before your God, your words were heard, and I have come in response to your words. But the prince of the kingdom of Persia was withstanding me for twenty-one days: then behold Michael, one of the chief princes, came to help me for I had been left there with the kings of Persia." This was speaking of the spiritual battle going on in Heaven as Daniel was praying.

The Israelites were set free soon after that.

There are many examples in the Bible that give illustrations of how God asked someone to pray or act upon something which would enable God's will to come to pass. Jesus even told us in Matthew 6:9-10 to pray that His kingdom would come and that His will would be done, on Earth as it is in Heaven. Why would Jesus ask us to pray this, if it was just going to happen? We are His representatives on Earth. He needs us to pray and ask for His perfect will to be accomplished.

Something else Dutch wrote that hit me hard was this: *"I can't help wondering how many promises from God have gone unfulfilled because He can't find the human involvement He needs."* [7]

After reading the first few chapters one evening, I knew God was speaking to my heart. I remember lying in my bed and committing to God that whatever He prompted me to pray for and walk ahead in, from that day forward, I would act upon and obey. I made a very serious and purposeful commitment to God that night. I told Him that I was ready to live this amazing life in partnership with Him in a more focused and deliberate way. I would be listening for His Holy Spirit to prompt me, and I would act.

Little did I know God was going to take me up on that, immediately. The very next morning was Mother's Day. In church, sitting with my three beautiful children and handsome husband, I have to say I felt like one very blessed woman. As all of the mothers were standing and being acknowledged by the pastor with a prayer and blessing (as well as carnations being given out), I was admiring all the other mothers around the room. Suddenly my eyes caught someone who stopped my heart in the moment. My gaze fell upon a woman and her husband who had been in the same ministry as Tim and me for the past few years. I knew they had been trying to have a baby for years but were unable to conceive. She was 44, and hope for her to conceive was coming close to the end.

I couldn't help but think how sad this day must be for them and how this little celebration must be so painful. Then something happened that I did not expect. At that moment, I felt like God spoke to my heart, asking me to go pray for her. As the thought came, I was in shock. "Oh no, that would not be a good idea. Here I am with three gorgeous children, and she has none." I argued with God that this would be a terrible thing, that it would just bring more pain for them today. "Any other day God, but not today. Not Mother's Day." I thought God's timing was totally off here.

Through the entire service I had my internal argument with God about this. At the end of the sermon I was almost physically sick over it all. I knew if I didn't just do it, my stomach could not take it physically. So I reluctantly went straight to them after church and asked them if I could pray for them. They graciously and sweetly said yes, completely oblivious to the fact that I was dying inside. As I prayed, I envisioned a picture of chains over her uterus. I prayed that God would release the chains that were keeping her from conceiving. As the prayer went on, I started to cry. Then she began to cry, and then none of us could talk. This was not going at all as I had anticipated it would. I wanted to just make small talk with her after the prayer and maybe help her feel comfortable about this whole thing. But oh no – we were all a mess!

At the end of the prayer I quickly hugged them goodbye through our tears, and then I headed straight to the bathroom to try to compose myself. In the bathroom stall I had some words to say to God. "Oh God, that was so not cool. I am so upset about that one. When I committed to say yes to whatever you prompted me with, you could have picked an easier scenario. Now I have really messed things up and made them cry. What a terrible thing to have made a mess of her emotions on this lovely Mother's Day." As I was having this conversation with God in my mind, I felt like He spoke to my heart and said, "Thank you for being obedient and saying yes." Even after that, I still felt crushed by it all.

When I got home from church, I tried calling the woman all day on the phone to try to apologize for causing her to cry and become emotional. I wanted to let her know it was not my intention at all, especially on Mother's Day. She never answered her phone that day, which only fed my insecurity. I didn't see her at work the next day, or the day after that. At that point, it became painful. On the third day, I finally saw her in the hallway. "Oh, Patricia (this woman's name has been changed to protect her anonymity)," I said. "I have been trying to get in touch with you. I felt so badly that I got all emotional when I was praying for you on Sunday." She stopped me mid-sentence and said, "Rebecca, I am so thankful that you prayed for us. We have been in the process of adopting from China, but the agency said there were red flags from my past preventing them from accepting our application. But I received news that in the last few days, they have agreed to accept our application, and we are approved to adopt a little boy." She pulled out a picture and showed me this sweet boy who they were trying to adopt. She continued to thank me for praying. "God is answering our prayers," she said.

Of course I was very happy for her, yet something inside of me said "This was not what I felt like God wanted me to pray for. I really felt God wanted to give her a baby from her womb." I was a bit confused but still wanted to share in their joyous news. My personal prayer for this couple continued to be for them to conceive, and all the while their adoption was going forward full throttle.

At Christmas time we went to Washington, and I had to make a business phone call to Patricia. As I was talking to her, she said, "Guess what? You are not going to believe this, but I am pregnant! We weren't telling anyone until I was at least three months along – and now I am, so we are letting everyone know! We are so shocked! We cannot believe this is actually happening." I said "Patricia, what about the adoption?" She said there was a couple who started fostering the little boy once the orphanage knew he had a family in America. They are an amazing couple who loved God, and they had fallen in love with this little boy. They had been begging to adopt him. Patricia said they wanted to wait until this baby was born before they made a final decision. She said, "I am too old to raise two babies at once. So I am seeing how God is taking care of all parties involved."

Six months later, an adorable, blue-eyed little boy with blond curly hair was born to this sweet couple. Every time I saw this little boy (up until age two when they moved up north) I would get all teary eyed. I don't take credit for the conception and birth of that little boy; I know many people were praying for this couple. Yet I have no doubt that God did something miraculous that Mother's Day. It was the beginning of my journey of saying yes – no matter what! What a privilege to be able to see this miracle unfold in front of me.

Because of the recovery steps I chose to take during this time of depression, I became empowered and willing to do whatever God asked. And because of that, I am seeing God do the miraculous as I walk forward. God blows me away daily. What a thrilling ride this life has become in partnership with God.

Brennan Manning sums this up in his book *Abba's Child*. *The recovery of passion begins with the recovery of my true self as the beloved. If I find Christ I find myself, and if I find my true self, I will find Him. This is the goal and purpose of our lives. John did not believe that Jesus was the most important thing; he believed that Jesus was the only thing. For "the disciple Jesus loved", anything less was not genuine faith.*

Questions for Personal Reflection:

- Is there something in your life that you feel you cannot overcome?

- Are you willing to take advice and get help if necessary (medically, professionally or spiritually)?

- What will it take to be free from this bondage in your life and to deal with your junk?

CHAPTER 10

POWER OVER DEATH

"Be of a sober spirit; be on the alert. Your adversary, the devil, prowls about like a roaring lion, seeking someone to devour."

– 1 Peter 5:7

Lying beside my desperately sick husband in a rustic hotel room with no doctor around was the most helpless feeling I had ever felt in my life.

Tim and I, with our three kids (then eleven, eight and six), were in Nicaragua leading a team of 25 young adults on a two-month field service in January 2000. Tim had begun to feel extremely worn out and run down, so we decided to get away for a few days. We picked a hotel on a beach a couple hours from where the team was staying. This would be a time for Tim to get some much-needed rest, and we could spend some quality family time with our kids on the beach. As we began to pack up for the trip, however, Tim started to feel sick. He was happy we were going to get away so he could rest and recover from whatever he was fighting.

After a two-hour drive, all crammed in a little taxi, we finally arrived. Tim said he felt worse and was just going to go to bed. After we checked into the hotel, he stayed in the room, and I took the kids for a fun time in the sand. The beach was breathtaking. Warm, humid air hit me as I breathed in the tropical setting. I love the heat, so this was a piece of paradise for me.

The kids were having a ball, and I was thankful for this restful place. My thoughts were never far from Tim though. I was wishing he felt better so he could enjoy this beautiful beach with us. Something inside me was not settled about Tim's sickness.

As the kids and I were eating dinner at the hotel restaurant, Tim hobbled down the stairway to meet us at our table. He looked terrible. He was only there for about 15 minutes when he began to feel nauseous. He thought he might throw up. He left the table and went straight back up to bed.

After dinner, the kids and I chased the crabs all up and down the shore as the bright moon lit up the whole beach. It was such a picturesque night. I was purposely stalling the kids, giving Tim time to fall into a deep sleep before I brought them to the room. I didn't want to disturb him when he felt so terrible.

When we finally came into the room, it looked like Tim was sound asleep. I was thankful for that. We tip-toed around the room very quietly so as not to disturb Tim's sleep. It was about 10 p.m. when the kids were finally all tucked in after their baths and showers. Tim rolled over and asked for some Tylenol. He tried to get back to sleep but said he was restless and just could not get comfortable.

The next morning, Tim still did not feel well. He tried to hang out on the beach with us, but he would sit for an hour or so then retreat back to the room to rest. The kids and I had another wonderful time on the beach, jumping waves, collecting seashells, walking to different areas and eating regularly at the restaurant in the hotel. Tim and I discussed going back to the city to get a doctor to look at him, but he said he would much rather stay here to rest than be back in the city. So the decision was made to stay.

The next day was more of the same for Tim. He still was not feeling well, and he wondered why the sickness was taking so much out of him. He concluded that he was just extra worn out, and his body was having a hard time fighting the flu-like symptoms. He also started to complain that all his joints and bones were really achy and sore; this was unlike what he had ever experienced before. Sometimes the pain would be so intense he said he could hardly stand it.

By the third evening Tim was not getting any better. In fact, I felt that he was getting much worse. I didn't want to seem like a worrier, but I just did not have a settled feeling, being so far away from any clinic in case we needed advanced care for Tim. And his bones being in so much pain just did not seem like a typical flu.

As I was getting the kids into bed that third night, Tim seemed to be sleeping through all the noisy proceedings of the kids' showers. When all was quiet, I lay beside Tim and suddenly realized something was seriously wrong. The bed was totally drenched with his sweat and he was burning up with fever. He moaned for me to get him some ibuprofen and Tylenol, as well as a cold washcloth for his head.

I told him that I was growing increasingly uncomfortable with the situation and recommended we leave the next day to get him to a doctor. He finally agreed, saying he really was in a lot of pain now and knew he needed a professional opinion. I was very worried about him at this point, particularly because of the sweating and high fever.

Around midnight, I was in a light sleep when Tim tapped me, moaning. "I feel horrible and not right," he said. "My whole body hurts, and my bones feel like they are broken. I feel like I need to throw up, but I can't even get out of bed. Can you please help me?" As I walked him to the bathroom, he was shaking uncontrollably, and sweat was dripping down his body. He stayed in the bathroom for a while then came back crawling to the bed.

Between one and two a.m., he was moaning in pain and still shaking. He said, "Something is really wrong with me. I am scared something is not right. I have never felt like this before." After saying that, he started going in and out of delirium – which really scared me. This was not a normal flu. My mind was racing, and all I could think about was finding help and getting Tim to a hospital immediately. This was way too scary for me to deal with on my own.

Being in Nicaragua in the middle of nowhere, getting medical attention was not a simple situation. I ran down to the hotel lobby and looked all around for someone to help me. No one was around. I looked at the phone and realized without speaking good Spanish, I couldn't even make a call. I picked up the phone, thinking maybe someone who knew English could help me, but that turned out to be futile. Cell phones were not common at that time, so we did not have one.

Then I thought – even if I did find someone to help me in the middle of the night, how could I get a taxi? No taxi drivers worked this late. It wasn't even safe to travel after dark in these areas, much less in the middle of the night. How would I even get my kids all packed up and into a little five-seat taxi when they were all sleeping? I couldn't leave my kids at the hotel with a total stranger; that was non-negotiable. Beyond that, even if we did get to the city in the middle of the night, no doctor works at those hours. Their hospitals are simply large clinics; they are not ones that are even equipped for emergency situations. This was clearly not where you want to be when you are horribly sick. The whole situation was crazy and seemed to be growing out of control the more I thought about it.

Even worse, I didn't think Tim could handle a two-hour taxi ride back to the city. He was delirious. He clearly was in trouble and needed help. I felt utterly and completely helpless.

As I went up to the room and lay beside my delirious husband, I was in complete despair and very scared for him. I cried out to God to help me know what to do. I have never felt so helpless in all my life.

I felt like God spoke very gently to my heart as I lay beside Tim. God prompted me to put my hands on him and just pray through the night for Him to spare Tim's life. As I prayed, Tim's moaning continued. I had heard different people say that when someone is dying you can sense death in the room. I never knew what that was until that night. I sensed death in the room all over Tim as I prayed for him in that very helpless situation. The delirium and sweats continued all night.

When sunlight shone through the windows in the wee hours of the morning, I rushed down the stairs to find help. I only found one person in the lobby. I pleaded with her to find a taxi as quickly as possible. We ended up having to wait quite a while for a taxi to arrive. Once it came, we threw everything in and headed straight to the city.

The taxi driver was very worried about Tim. He told me over and over that my husband was very sick and that I needed to take him straight to the hospital. He kept apologizing for his old taxi not being able to go any faster. When we finally made it to the city, I was so relieved to be able to walk through the process of starting to identify what was really wrong with my husband. The hospital in the city was not much more than a clinic but at that point I was thankful for any help we could get.

The doctor performed many different tests, and we sat for what seemed like hours in the waiting room. When the doctor came out he had a very solemn face. A 12-year-old boy came with us to translate, and when the doctor told the boy what to tell us all that the boy could say was, "Oh, this is bad. This is very bad. Oh, wow." I begged him to just tell us. He said, "Your husband has the worst strand of dengue fever called hemorrhagic dengue.[8] This is the one that kills many people here." Then he proceeded to tell us all the people he knew who had died from this, which did not help relieve our concerns in any way.

The doctor explained in detail about that particular strand. It makes your blood platelet count so low that you can begin to bleed to death internally because your blood does not have the ability to clot. He said if this happened in Nicaragua you could hemorrhage to death internally. Nicaragua did not have the ability to give blood transfusions, so it was fatal. He also said that Tim's platelet count was so low that if he fell or cut himself shaving or hurt himself in any way, his blood did not have enough platelets to clot and therefore he would bleed to death.

He gave Tim strict orders to stay in bed all day (which was fine, since he was too weak to do anything else). He also told Tim not to do anything that would cause him to bruise or bleed.

This sickness is also called the "bone-crushing disease". For some reason, every bone in your body has such severe pain that it sometimes feels as if all your bones are being crushed. It is very painful to endure with no treatment. The disease is contracted through a mosquito bite. Unlike malaria, where you can take anti-malarial medicine and be treated, there is no prevention or treatment for hemorrhagic dengue. He basically had to wait and see if his body would either recover or hemorrhage.

I later found out you can also die from shock if your blood pressure drops too low, which is what I believe was happening in that hotel room when Tim was going in and out of delirium.

The doctor looked at me and somberly said, "Please take all my advice very seriously. Your husband will die if his platelet count goes any lower." I asked if we could fly Tim out of Nicaragua so that he could get a blood transfusion in

America if needed. But the doctor told us if Tim flew with his low platelet count, he would hemorrhage to death on the plane due to the air pressure fluctuation. That was not even an option.

Upon getting this information I emailed many friends and family to pray for Tim. Over the next three weeks in Nicaragua, Tim's platelet count slowly began to rise. I know that the prayers of so many people around the world are what saved his life. God answered all our prayers. After 40 days in bed and countless hours of uncertainty, Tim was able to recover. It actually took Tim close to five years to regain his full health again.

Through this experience, I started to understand God's power over death and over impossible situations. My faith rises up every time I recount the details of this experience. I am so thankful that God walks through these very dark places with us and shows His power when we least expect we are going to need Him.

In a time when I could have felt so alone, I knew God was there. I was still scared, but my fear turned to peace when I resolved that, no matter what, I was going to trust in Him. I had no other choice. **I was either going to plunge into great despair, or I was going to trust my Maker to take care of us – however He chose to do that.** In the hotel room, God's prompting was simply to put my hand on my husband's sweaty back and breathe prayers of healing and life over his body.

As Tim and I travel through different parts of Africa, we stumble upon very difficult and impossible situations. In these situations it has been so amazing to be able to cry out to God for His intervention and to see Him literally come through with miracle after miracle and provision after provision, as we reach out in desperation. I often think of those who do not have God to cry out to, and how hopeless many circumstances would be without Him. Thank you, God, for being so real and present in all circumstances of our life!

There have only been a few times since this experience that I have ever felt the same spirit of death in my room. One situation that comes to mind was when I was in Benin, West Africa on a trip to visit an orphanage we had been helping for a couple of years.

None of my trips to Benin have been easy. With all the Voodoo and witchcraft that exist in the country, there are always many interesting things that happen when we show up to help the kids who have no hope for survival without someone intervening into their lives. There are many things that I have to address on each of these trips, and sometimes a few of the locals are not too happy with me.

One issue I addressed was convincing the government in a certain area up north to create laws making sure that an orphan who dies is issued a death certificate. I wanted to make sure that an orphan was not just buried in someone's back yard, without some record of how that child died and who that child was. In this area of Benin, an orphan has no value, and most locals see no need to have a death certificate made for orphan children when they die. One lady literally said to me, "Who would care if an orphan dies? They do not belong to anyone, so no one would really care why they died." All kinds of abuses happen to these kids, and most people do not even acknowledge that this goes on. Advocating for a death certificate puts a stake in the ground to claim that this child is a human being, regardless of whether there are parents in the equation. So I made this a big deal.

In one particular orphanage home, I had come with a team who was ready to go to work. In preparation for the trip, I made nametags for each of the children in the home so we could better remember their names. Upon passing the nametags out, we discovered that 16 children were missing. When I approached the director about this, he simply stated that those 16 children had died that year. To my shock and horror, I repeated my question, not feeling like he understood. Yet he continued to stick with his same answer and said, "No, they have all died."

So my investigation began. For a whole week in confrontation after confrontation, this director stood by his story that all the children had died. Since no record is needed for dead orphan children, there was no proof either way. By the end of the week, after my own investigation, I had full evidence that they were not dead. At this point I brought the local social welfare department into the picture.

In Benin, a country known for large child trafficking numbers, I felt it was very important to get to the bottom of what really happened to those children.

I set up a time to bring a social welfare representative and the mayor's representative down with me to confront the orphanage director with the evidence. We would do this to try to bring truth to the matter. One of my friends named Kathy and another friend named Hope, who served as my translator, were also with me at the time. We went to the orphanage and let the director know that the next day we were bringing the government officials to speak to him. We told him that these children would have to be accounted for; either we would be taken to their gravesite with full explanation of how they died, or we would be given full disclosure of what really happened to them.

When he got this news, he was furious that I would go this far. I once again gave him the chance to tell us the full truth of the whereabouts of the children he said were dead, but again he stuck by his story. So my friends and I left saddened by this web of deceit.

In this particular area, when someone gets very angry with you and doesn't want you around anymore, they do not just tell you to go away. They instead 'put a curse' on you or poison you. They have found this to be much easier than confrontation. Their intention is for you to get very sick or even die, depending on what kind of threat you pose to them. It is very interesting that in this area no one confronts justice or human rights issues, or any other issue that could cause a disagreement, because no one wants to make a conflict with anyone. They all fear being cursed. Every family has a story of how an auntie died from such and such a curse. Or a brother is sick because he was cursed. The list is endless of the curses that have crippled these families.

Now I know many of you reading this will be saying to yourself, "Well, they may believe it is a curse, but isn't it really just a normal sickness, a normal thing this person died of? I mean, in Africa, everyone thinks that sicknesses are a curse." Yes, that is the case for many of the illnesses and deaths, but I also know now from personal experience that the power of these curses are very real, and that without being able to call on the name of Jesus, we too would become victims in these areas. Oh, how thankful I am for the power that we have in Christ! I am always praying for extra protection for myself as well as for those who I am traveling with. I do not personally walk in any fear of these curses. I know that God is so much greater than any of this. But I am also no dummy to realities of the spiritual realm. I know that Satan is alive and is out to kill, steal and destroy anything he is allowed to touch. So I am extra cautious not to walk forward in naivety either. In 1 Peter 5:7, it says, "Be of a sober spirit; be on the alert. Your adversary, the devil, prowls about like a roaring lion, seeking someone to devour." It also says in Ephesians 6:12 that "we are not wrestling against flesh and blood, but against principalities and powers of darkness."

For anyone who questions if we are really living in a spiritual battlefield of good versus evil, my advice to you would be to go and visit some of these very dark places. After just a short time there, you will not have any question left in your mind that this spiritual battle is very real.

After my encounter with this particular orphanage director, my friend and I went to dinner with our other teammates. Before we all retired for bed, a few of us got together to pray for the kids in the area, as well as for wisdom to know how to go forward with the different tasks we wanted to accomplish while there. We also prayed that the truth would come out in this whole matter.

As my friend Kathy and I went to bed that night, we were both completely exhausted. We each climbed into our very uncomfortable beds and tucked our mosquito nets deep under our mattresses to make sure we were protected for the night from all the mosquitoes. I listened to a few songs on my CD player and then began to give in to my exhaustion.

As I was lying there, completely wiped out and trying to sleep, I suddenly felt a dark presence in the room. It was dark and spooky. I prayed under my breath for it to go away, but no prayer seemed to make it leave. I decided to ignore it, in case it was just in my mind. As I tried again to fall asleep, to my horror, I had a very clear and distinct impression that the presence tried to suck the breath out of my mouth. I gasped for air and realized that this dark presence I was sensing was very real. I felt completely paralyzed in my bed and could not move. I remember saying the name of Jesus in my mind, but I could not voice anything aloud. I had never experienced anything like this. It was absolutely paralyzing and terrifying.

I prayed hard in my mind, and then I tried to ignore this presence of darkness, but it would not go away. I thought if I could just get to sleep, it would disappear. So I tried again to fall asleep, but as I drifted off, again I would feel the breath being sucked out of my mouth. I would gasp for air and then try it all over again. Each time, I felt that if I did fall into a deep sleep, my breath would be taken from me and I would die. It was evident this spirit in my room wanted to take my life.

As the night went on, I sensed the same spirit of death that was in the hotel room in Nicaragua the night I was praying for my husband. I tried to get out of my mosquito net so I could walk to my friend Kathy's bed and ask her to pray for me. I wanted to make her aware of what I was going through, but I could not even get out of my bed. I would envision myself lifting my net and walking over to her, but I could not physically do it. It was like a bad nightmare, but I knew I was completely awake and it was all really happening.

By five a.m., the light started shining into the window and suddenly I didn't feel the presence in the room anymore. As I lay there, tears rushed down my face as I acknowledged how grateful I was that Satan has no say in whether I live or die. **It is God who has my every breath in His hands, and He is the only one who has the right to say when I live or die.** I really felt that if I did not have God in my life, I would not have lived through that night. The dark side of the spirit world was very real, and it was evident that someone wanted me out of the picture.

I slept for a couple hours and then told Kathy what had happened. She said she also had a horrible sleep, that she was agitated and restless with nightmares all night. She was equally upset about our night of terror and distress.

That morning we went to the orphanage for the confrontational meeting. Upon arrival, the director looked at me with shock on his face, almost as if he was seeing a ghost. In noticing his reaction to my entrance, it instantly dawned on me that he very well could have been the one who had cursed me. It would certainly be consistent with what happens when you confront someone in that area. My friends from the government then showed up, and the orphanage director confessed that the children were not dead. He said they had run away, and that he didn't want me spending all my time on my visit looking for them, so that is why he had told me they were dead.

To this day, we have not found out the full truth of what happened to the children, but we continue to bring the government into each situation to address issues of deceit and neglect. This particular director no longer has a legal license to run an orphanage because of the many issues that were uncovered with his negligent care-taking.

About a year and a half ago, a 24-year-old female American Peace Corp volunteer in Benin was killed, not far from where we worked. Her throat was slit in the middle of the night. To many in the western world, her death was a mystery. No one could figure out why someone would do this to a sweet young lady who was making such a difference in the village where she was working. To most of us who regularly work in those areas of Benin, however, it was quite obvious that she was most likely killed because she brought up justice issues or made someone feel threatened by her presence.

Now, over a year later, the mother of this volunteer is speaking out to say that she knows why her daughter was murdered, even though the Peace Corps investigators' findings have been inconclusive so far. She said her daughter was teaching English at a local school and learned some of the kids were being sexually abused by one of the teachers. She was asked to help them by some of the female staff. A few days after anonymously reporting the abuser, she turned up dead. Her mother feels that this is what led to her murder.

Each time I remember this story, I am brought back to the reality that this is exactly what I am doing in a much larger scale each time I go back to Benin. I know my life is threatened due to the magnitude of the issues I am addressing daily while there. Many are happy I am addressing these injustice issues, but some are not. I have curses directed at me regularly, and I know some would like me dead. My strength lies in knowing who has my last breath in His hands. When God says my life is over, then it will be over – but until then, I will continue to fight this fight for the justice of the children. If we won't fight for them, who will?

Ultimately, we need God to cover our every action in life. As I look ahead, I am choosing to live with purpose each day. **May all my energy and my every breath be used for Christ's purposes to see lives transformed and the hurting set free – domestically and internationally!** That is what I call really living. None of us know how long we have to live on this Earth. Let's live to the fullest and with purpose.

Questions for Personal Reflection:

- Are you prepared to die today?

- What keeps you from being ready?

- If you knew you only had six months left to live, would you live your life differently?

~~~~~~~~~~~~~~~~

DETERMINED NOT TO
FORGET

~~~~~~~~~~

"Our lives begin to end the day we become silent about things that matter."

— *Martin Luther King Jr.*

L iberia sits on Africa's western coast and is classified as one of the continent's least developed countries. A brutal civil war between 1989 and 2003 destroyed a nation already struggling to maintain minimal services for its citizens. Liberia's fragile economy was destroyed and hardly a person in the entire nation was not adversely affected in some manner. Many businessmen and industry leaders fled during the war, taking much of the country's capital and expertise with them.

As a result of the war, clinics and hospitals across the country were destroyed. [9]

"Liberia is unique in all of Africa," explains Pamela White, Mission Director for USAID Liberia. "This is partly because of the disastrous civil war that burned every clinic, school, electrical supply and water main. During that time there were no schools or jobs or places for children to be safe. When you have seen the horrors that occurred here, you are never 'normal' again."

Some estimates suggest there were nearly 5,000 children living in the country's orphanages after the war. [10] Not all of Liberia's orphans are without parents – as much as 70% of them may have been abandoned by families unable to cope with another mouth to feed.

Children were an integral part of both government and rebel armies in Liberia during the war. Reports show that child soldiers could have made up 25-75% of the total fighting forces in Liberia. [11] According to a 2003 report from the Council on Foreign Relations, which was compiled after many of Liberia's civil war atrocities were brought to light, "Boys, as well as girls, were either kidnapped or conscripted by armed groups. Many were drugged, with everything from liquor and marijuana to gun powder mixed into milk or cocaine rubbed into cuts on their faces."

Many children saw their loved ones killed in front of them, or were kidnapped and threatened with death if they didn't join the violence. Experts agree that without focused intervention aimed at reintegrating them into society, child soldiers – who have witnessed and participated in the worst atrocities of war in Liberia and elsewhere – have little chance of rejoining normal civilian life.

After the end of the civil war, a level of peace was restored to the country and in 2006 the first female President, Ellen Johnson Sirleaf came into office. She has been a great asset to the country and is also gaining an increasing level of recognition on the world stage due to her engaging personality and effective policies of reunification and development. She is aggressively campaigning against corruption and is working very hard to bring the country back to health after the 14 years of civil war.

There was no running water or electricity anywhere in the country when we first arrived in 2005; now in 2011, they are just starting to get these things up and running again in the capital.

Coming back to America in 2006 after living in Africa for almost two years was a difficult transition. Yes, it was definitely great to come back to all the conveniences of the western world, yet there were other things that were not very easy to return to. I experienced reverse culture shock. I looked at things very differently after living in the poorest areas of Africa.

On our flight back, I picked up a magazine at the airport and read about a certain celebrity who spent over $100,000 on her daughter's first birthday party that month. I couldn't help but think about what we had just been able to do with a quarter of that amount at Fatu's orphanage, which changed the future of over 80 children's lives. With approximately $27,000 we were able to dig a well for clean drinking water, build toilets, showers, a new roof, a kitchen, flooring, and we got beds and mosquito nets for many of the children to keep them safe while sleeping. These children were in great misery and suffering horribly before our intervention.

Soon after arriving home we were invited to a Super Bowl party. Before the game came on, the TV announcer discussed how much money was being spent to put on all the Super Bowl festivities. The amounts were in the millions. Different commercials alone were costing businesses a million dollars for a 30 second ad during the game.

My heart sank as I tried to process these amounts spent on one afternoon of entertainment. Millions of dollars were being wasted on something so temporary. It was hard to accept, knowing that across the world in Africa, 35,000 people die each day due to hunger-related ailments. Couldn't we think of a better use for our resources to help the world around us than spending such amounts on our simple forms of entertainment? I know I am now ruffling a few feathers (especially all of you sports fans), but this was how I was impacted after having had that level of involvement in the lives of those who are at the very bottom of the poverty barrel.

A challenge to consider would be the difference we can all make in this world by just looking around us to help those in need with our wealth and surplus instead of spending it on things that are so superficial. **We all have the power to relieve someone's suffering through our resources.**

Watching financial waste was not easy – and still is not – yet in seeing all this I made a conscious decision not to get judgmental. I have decided not to waste my energy judging others but to focus my efforts into personally being proactive to help those in my path, however I can do that, and inspiring others to do the same. Doing my part and letting God do the rest is how I go forward. It is none of my business how others choose to use their finances and resources, but it is my business how I spend mine.

As Tim and I would try to sleep in our comfortable, soft bed, which I absolutely melt in, we would lay awake at night thinking of the many suffering children in Africa's orphanages. We knew many would not have a future without outside intervention after what we had just experienced. The children now had faces and stories that we were personally aware of.

The number of Liberian orphanages in Fatu's same condition haunted us at night: at that time there were 79 in this uncertified category, without the prospect of assistance to overcome their manifold obstacles. There was so much needless suffering. Our minds could not rest. The words of Rick Warren continued to come back to me daily. *"When God gives you a burden, feed it. Don't ignore it. Let it break your heart."*

So Tim and I did. We let ourselves remember the faces, the stories, the awful suffering of innocent children and hopeless situations. We let our hearts break when we thought about all the little children crying themselves to sleep at night because their bellies were hungry. We thought about the lifeless bodies of those who have no hope unless someone helps them.

As we did this, we started to sense what God was saying in our hearts. We must never forget. We must act and fight for these kids' lives and futures through actions and not just through words.

We can all tell great stories, yet if we are not willing to put prayers, muscles and finances behind those stories, they accomplish nothing!

We were feeling specifically called to help the orphans in the homes that no other organization would touch. They were the homes in the worst conditions with children living in the most complicated situations.

With these promptings, we began processing how to help as many suffering orphan children as possible in the appalling orphanage homes. We came up with ways to avoid being used by corrupt directors and help the legitimate, honest directors, all along utilizing every dollar and resource to its fullest. God's prompting in our hearts led us to start in Liberia.

We put plans together creating self-sustainable answers for the homes so we would not create long-term dependency on ourselves. Our eight previous years with Mercy Ships and ten-year business experience played to our advantage.

Mercy Ships founders Don and Deyon Stephens gave us their full blessing to launch out on our own with this new ministry that we knew God was calling us to. We are so grateful for this couple. They have been great examples to us throughout their years of serving the poor and needy. We are so thankful for the opportunities they gave us to serve in many different capacities in our eight years serving alongside them.

Moving forward, we brainstormed with our close friend and previous co-worker Matt Le Page about putting a plan of action together to start an organization that would respond to the needs we had been exposed to in Africa. We considered linking with other orphan aid groups but could not find any of them willing to take a risk on the most complicated homes. We also found that we would be restricted to working within their rules and regulations, and we knew there was no rulebook on how to handle the myriad of challenges we were anticipating in each individual home. We would have to create our own rulebook as we went along.

We had to start somewhere, and after much deliberation we made the decision to call the movement Orphan Relief and Rescue. We were approached by some friends to bring this dream under their organization so that we could begin immediate service to the kids in Africa. This collaborate venture with Sharing International would cut out the immediate headache of having to create a new organization right away. They said we could see how it worked out, and at a later time, they could help us file for our own non-profit status if we wanted to do that.

After processing and praying, we felt strongly that we were to accept Sharing International's offer so we could begin immediately with no significant start-up costs. We could put every dollar raised into the work on the field to help the needy kids right away.

We also recruited four qualified individuals who were completely trustworthy and who were able to raise their own financial support. After a short preparation time in Texas they were ready to be taken to Liberia to begin the dream of Orphan Relief and Rescue.

Tim and I felt we needed to live in America with our three kids to establish a support base in the West, as well as to raise awareness for the huge needs of the children in Liberia and Benin. Both he and I would take turns traveling to Africa to oversee what was going on in the field.

We had many financial obstacles come up as we were planning our first deployment to Liberia to orient the team. Meanwhile, God continued to make it very clear to each of us that we were to move forward with the date of flight we had agreed upon.

This was a very scary time for Tim and I and even our whole family, to a greater extent. It is one thing to have God-given experiences shape a vision for reaching out to His beloved creation – it is another to put the proverbial stake in the ground and intentionally put aside a pursuit for gainful employment to take steps toward living by faith and completely trusting God to provide. We could never have done it without the guidance of dear friends and co-workers, as well as faithful prayer partners.

With only $3,400 raised to take with us, we boarded the plane to Monrovia, Liberia's capital. This was a total faith walk for all of us. I looked around at the team members God had brought us, and my heart was full and thankful. Each of them is a humble and caring individual with an amazing servant's heart. Matt Le Page is a dear friend who is skilled in fixing pretty much anything. He came as our mechanical engineer from Guernsey, UK. Mariel Besmer, (who later married Matt Le Page), is a nurse and has a huge heart of compassion for the suffering. Andrew Tyler is a very gifted and skilled man in logistics and carpentry with a heart to do whatever is needed of him. Matthew Cramer (who helped build George Sr.'s house) is talented in many different areas logistically, as well as in video editing and communications. We also had our Liberian friend named Morris, who worked with us on Fatu's home and was waiting on the ground for us when we arrived.

It had been about 10 months since I was last in Liberia. As I walked off the plane, the warm, humid air hit my body and I instantly felt at home. It was so great to be back. I was excited to see what God was going to do in the weeks ahead!

We stayed with friends while putting the organizational plans together. We hit the ground running with meeting after meeting. We felt incredible favor with each person and government official we met. Early indicators pointed to a favorable reception to the work that was on our hearts to accomplish.

The staff members at the Ministry of Social Welfare were very excited to see us back in their country. The word was already around the government offices about the transformation of Fatu and Sebastion Smith's home. We had immediate favor and credibility with them. They knew we had done this first project while with Mercy Ships, so we shared that we were now under a new organization that would specifically focus on orphanage work as a unique entity. We also had many Liberian friends advise us culturally as we moved forward. Many of them led frequent prayer meetings to pray for us as we were setting up all the details. We had so much emotional and spiritual support. I regularly told my Liberian friends that it was their prayers that were going to make the difference for their people. Our success with helping them was going to come as they prayed. And oh, did they ever pray.

One main hardship when we arrived was our dependency on borrowed vehicles and taxis, which were unreliable mechanically. This became very frustrating because of the frequent breakdowns and flat tires. I was so tired of wasting countless hours because of unpredictable vehicles. Our guys ended up under more vehicles than they were in because of these issues.

One evening, a week into the trip, I was lying in bed in total distress over the vehicle situation. I called Fatu and asked her to pray for us and especially for my attitude. I hated not having the finances to buy a vehicle, and I felt pretty helpless under the circumstances with just $3,400 in our pocket. I knew this amount would just cover our room and board at the guesthouse, as well as secure a rental home for the team.

When I shared this with Fatu, she said, "Yes I will pray, and God will provide. You are not asking selfishly Rebecca; you only want to help the orphan children here. So God will provide. You will see." While in bed, still frustrated, I felt God speak to my heart that we were right where He wanted us to be. The sense came to me that this was how God wanted us to come into the country – completely dependent on Him and dependent on the Liberians to help us bring aid to their own people. It was critical for them not to see us come in with the big bucks due to their perception of all the westerners (Americans and Europeans). They think we are all wealthy and have limitless amounts of money at our disposal.

It was important for them to see the need to pray very hard for God to bring our organization into existence. This was exactly what God had in mind for Orphan Relief and Rescue at the beginning. The Liberians needed to have ownership and feel that they were playing a critical role in the foundation of this organization. Then, as larger finances came in, all our friends, children and orphanage directors would know that this was truly God's provision and dream.

I didn't like this impression, yet I was getting a glimpse of what God's intention was for us. "Okay God," I said. "It's all great that we are to come in humbly and dependent, but I need to get some things done before I fly out, and the team is depending on me to help them. So please work this whole car thing out." Completely discouraged, I went to sleep, leaving it in God's hands.

The next morning, we had a VIP vehicle show up at our door with a driver, asking for Rebecca Pratt. The team came to my room and said there was someone there to see me. I went outside and greeted the driver. I introduced myself to him and asked him what I could help him with. He said, "My name is Victor, and I am here to take you wherever you want to go for the week." I looked at him in total amazement. "Really? Wow! And who can I thank for the use of this vehicle?" Victor told me, "You can thank former President Blah. This is his personal vehicle." Of course I had a million more questions at that moment, but we also had many more meetings to go to. So we all loaded in the vehicle, and off we went in our answer to prayer.

While driving down the road, I asked Victor if I could call former President Blah to thank him for the use of his vehicle. Victor said, "No, you cannot just call him on your phone because the Secret Service will not let you through to talk to him. But I will call him on my phone, and then you can talk to him." So I called him via Victor's phone and thanked him for his provision.

Later in the week, we went to thank him personally. As we drove up to his home, we saw armed guards with all their weaponry at the top of his security tower checking us out as we entered his compound. Victor explained that this was normal because of all the death threats he got on a regular basis. He had to have 24-hour armed guards to protect him and his family.

Upon arrival, it was clear that at one time this home was the pride of the country, but after the civil war, the scarce resources available made it a home in need of many repairs. Once inside, we were welcomed by former First Lady Nettie Blah, and soon after former President Blah joined us. We immediately felt welcomed as he was so kind and friendly.

He sat down and told us how he became aware of our need for a vehicle that week. He said it was Fatu who had called him, pleading with him to loan his vehicle to us for the week because of our situation. He said, "Rebecca, Fatu is like a daughter to me. She worked with me as my religious advisor in my presidency. She prayed for my family and me every day. She helped us get through so much. It was actually her and my wife's prayers that brought me to God. I can never repay what she has done for my family and me. When her kids were hungry and in distress, I had nothing to give; the war had just ended. I was not even being paid for my position in the country. I was so grieved we could not help her. You have no idea how difficult it was to watch her and her kids suffer like they did. We would send some food when we could. Then you came in and brought food and medicine and renovated their whole home. You were the answer to all our prayers for Fatu. So for that, we are so grateful. Whatever we can do to help you, we want to do that. I don't have power in the government anymore, or financial means, but you do have my friendship from here on out. I am indebted to you and your team as a friend, Rebecca." He then thanked us for coming back to his country to help the many more orphans who are suffering just like Fatu and her children were.

While he was speaking, my eyes were teary as I realized that what we do affects not only those we are helping in front of us but also all those who are watching and who love these suffering ones. We have no idea of the web of blessing we are weaving as we help others.

Each day when Victor arrived to take us to the various meetings and orphanage appointments, I was so in awe of God's provision. I remember only getting one flat tire with Victor, caused by the bad roads. This was such a gift and such a relief after all of the grief experienced with the borrowed cars and taxis.

We were able to accomplish everything on my list before I had to leave the team to go back to my own family in America. We secured a permanent home for the team to live in and acquired many things necessary for the team to begin their work. It did take another couple of months to secure a team vehicle because of having to raise more funds before one could be purchased, but our team had a good attitude in spite of all the obstacles. They are the first to say that this beginning time was not easy. However, in processing with them regularly, I can honestly say they were very faithful to all that God asked them to walk through to be able to help so many children who were in great distress.

Sharing International has since helped us launch out on our own. Donald Clark, who was the Vice President of Sharing International at that time, has been key in helping us with all of the paperwork and accounting procedures to make this possible. He has now come to work with Orphan Relief and Rescue full time as our CFO and business advisor. This man has been such a gift and has facilitated the existence of our work. He and his wife Andrea have been incredibly selfless in all their endeavors to help the children and us. We are humbled by their lives daily.

This was the beginning of seeing justice come to pass for countless children through taking action in response to God's relentless promptings in our hearts.

Questions for Personal Reflection:

- In what area of your life do you lack trust in God?

- Can God trust you to follow through with whatever He asks of you, even if the resources seem quite small?

- Are you using your money and resources wisely so that you can help others in need?

CHAPTER 12

USHERING JUSTICE IN

*"You see, Africa makes a fool of our idea of justice.
It makes a farce of our idea of equality. It mocks
our pieties. It doubts our concern. It questions our
commitment. Because there is no way we can look
at what's happening in Africa, and if we're honest,
conclude that it would ever be allowed to happen
anywhere else."*

– Bono

*"All that it takes for evil to succeed is for good men
to do nothing!"*

– Edmund Burke

Horrific screams were heard all through the neighborhood. It sounded as if someone was being given the most terrible beating. One by one, the neighbors followed the noise until they arrived at the scene. They could hardly believe their eyes; an uncle was taking all his anger out on a boy and girl around the ages of 13 and 14. They were being beaten profusely with no mercy. As the neighbors arrived, the uncle would scream at them just go away; this was none of their business. According to him, the children deserved what they were getting, and the neighbors just needed to stay out of it.

By this time, the children had whip marks all over their bodies. A friend of mine arrived home from work a couple of hours after the beatings had begun. This scene was going on right next to her home.

My friend immediately asked her house help and daughter what the screams were about next door. They informed her that the beatings had been going on for the last couple of hours and that they had tried to put a stop to it with no success. My friend, being involved in children's justice issues, was mortified at the ordeal. She stormed over to the home and pleaded with the man to stop for fear that he was going to kill these innocent children. He screamed back at her that it was none of her business and that she needed to go. These children were his responsibility, and she needed to stay out of it.

Through the yelling and hollering of both my friend and the uncle, the story came out that the girl and boy were his niece and nephew, from two different families. One child was from his side and one from his wife's. The children lived in their small two-room home and were used as their domestic help to care for the man, his wife and their two-year old baby. The scandal began when the niece's stomach started showing, and it came to light that the nephew had gotten her pregnant. The uncle said he was going to beat this out of them and they were never going to humiliate him and his family again.

Throughout the beatings, he would have the children lay on their backs and then on their fronts, wearing only their underwear, until their bodies were covered in deep welts. The pregnant teenage girl had whip marks all over her stomach and breasts. It was a sight unimaginable to witness, especially in light of her pregnancy.

After being unsuccessful with the uncle, my friend ran home and called her friend, who was a neighborhood leader, and pleaded with her to do something. She suggested she call the police and see if they would intervene.

Upon calling the police, she was informed that they would not come. They told her they would not get involved in a domestic dispute. This whole situation was unbearable to witness. My friend knew if she was in the main city of Cotonou, Benin, the police would have come immediately, but where she lived in the rural area the cultural norms were more complicated.

The beatings went on for several hours. Early the next morning, a relative came and picked up the children. At least they lived through this beating. But for my friend, it left an indelible impression that she would not forget any time soon.

On my recent trip to Benin this same friend picked me up from the airport. She was not in the mood for small talk at the beginning, as she was greatly burdened by what she had just witnessed. She said, "Rebecca, I have to tell you what happened recently that has really affected me. I am still traumatized over it all, and I have to tell you about it." As she explained the horror of what happened to the two children at the hands of their uncle, she said, "More safe homes need to be built for the children who are being severely abused and who are disadvantaged orphans. I have often heard many children have no value in a home when a relative takes them in, but now I have seen it first-hand. I have often questioned if an institutional setting is the right place for children who are used as a domestic servant because they are orphaned or impoverished. I used to think they might be better off in their families' homes – even if they are treated as domestic servants; but I don't think that anymore after what I have seen. And there is no doubt in my mind that putting them in a safe home or orphanage setting is literally rescuing them. This man had no concern for these children. They were as good as dead to him. More needs to be done, Rebecca."

I knew I had to genuinely listen to what she was saying because this was not her typical belief system. We are both in agreement that finding good loving homes for children with their own relatives is the best scenario. Yet sometimes this just is not possible. It is very difficult to find relatives who will not treat them like slaves, particularly the true orphans.

As she described the neighbors' responses, we talked about the reasons behind the neighbors' reactions and how it was possible for them to ignore the issues in front of them. I looked at my friend and said, "May God give us wisdom on how to help more children in these distressing situations."

At the end of my couple weeks in Benin, this friend took me to the top of her roof and said she wanted to show me something. When we arrived at the top, I was amazed at the beautiful view of the entire neighborhood. She pointed out where the beating took place and then proceeded to point out white flags on the roofs of different homes. "See all those flags?" she asked. "That is where all the people who are high up in the Voodoo world live. They put those white flags on top of their homes for anyone who needs help putting a curse on someone. People can come to them, and they will mix up the right potion or walk them through how to put a specific curse on someone to bring on a sickness, loss of a job or even death. That is what we have to deal with here, and that is why no one in my neighborhood would dare to get involved when the children were beaten. No one wanted to be cursed by this man." "Wow," I breathed. "There are quite a few of these flags around. No wonder they are living in such fear. That is why we are here," I said. This was the beginning of what is now a major focus of our work – advocating for justice on behalf of the many voice-less children in terrible circumstances.

Princess was a quiet, sweet girl who was being used as a domestic servant in an orphanage home in Liberia where we were dropping off food. Through our conversations with the children and particularly Princess, our field nurse found out she was being severely abused physically and verbally by the orphanage director. It also came to our attention that the social welfare office had closed down an orphanage home he had run previously due to allegations that he had been sexually abusing the children. Now he was running this home and continued to abuse kids under a different ministry name.

When this was brought to our attention, we worked with the social welfare office, giving them all the information they needed to remove this particular girl and close this man down once and for all. They started by transferring Princess to a different home.

Princess was very scared through the whole process, yet she was thankful she would be safe. Our field nurse was great with her –making every effort to ensure she felt comfortable in her new home.

The social welfare office submitted a letter of closure to the orphanage home a few days later, making it illegal for them to have children other than their own biological ones in the home.

We at Orphan Relief and Rescue would like to see this man in jail for what he has done, but without physical evidence, this has been a difficult thing to prove. Our laws for protection of women and young girls are much more advanced here in the United States. We are working hard alongside the social welfare office to make sure that this man cannot have children in his care ever again. Bringing justice to the many children who are being abused by very neglectful and abusive directors is a top priority for us as we help children in various capacities.

Through our food relief program, we are able to evaluate many directors. We find out quickly which ones are using their kids for selfish purposes. Many abuses occur under those directors. We also find directors who truly care about their kids and are loving parents yet simply do not have the resources to take care of their children adequately.

Unfortunately, we see way too many of those directors I would categorize as evil, ones who should never be allowed to have children in their care. These directors are selfishly using the kids as a business so they will get pity from foreigners who are easily conned into believing their many deceptions. I am always running into fellow humanitarians who are fully supporting some of these very awful directors, and my heart sinks as I hear the stories of how they have been conned into giving so much – yet nothing ever reaches the kids. The tragedies are great. I am always begging people to do their homework on these directors before dishing out any money, or they will most likely end up very disappointed and disillusioned. One should never assume that all orphanage directors have good and compassionate hearts. That is the first mistake most people from the West make all too often.

We are working to bring change to this situation. After many years of facing the challenges of Liberia's orphanages and the multitude of complicated issues, we now have an active role in Liberia's Child Protection Network. This task force is charged with preventing and addressing abuse and child trafficking. Along with the local government and the United Nations, we are taking an aggressive, proactive approach to protecting and advocating for these children. We are also working with the local governments in Benin on these same issues.

We feel that to make a long-term difference in children's lives in Africa, we have to partner with the local government's social welfare offices. We have to be an asset and help them be successful in their endeavors as we encourage them along in making some tough decisions. When these abusive directors are discovered, we share all the information we have with the social welfare office to see these homes closed once and for all and the children removed. We are seeing some real results, yet we are also seeing that a lot more needs to be done.

We make ourselves available as a resource of information about how to go about helping homes for anyone who wants to do work in African orphanages. This is a learned process and people need to be guided in these endeavors.

Esther and I hugged and cried together as we sat on her bottom bunk bed. I explained again why I could not take her home to America with me. "Do you remember when I first met you six years ago and how sick you were? Do you remember how your stomach hurt badly because you were so hungry?" I asked. She shook her head yes, eyes dripping with tears. "Think of how you are doing now and how wonderful your life has been since we helped you." I looked her in the eyes and said, "Esther, you know I love you, right?" She looked up and shook her head yes. "If I take you home with me, then I would not be able to help the many other children here who are suffering like you were. Keeping you here pushes me to always come back to make sure you are okay. If I leave you here, I am able to focus on fighting for you and for all the other needy kids who are so desperate for someone to help them. I need to continue fighting. Will you allow me to do that? You will always be my special girl, but I need you to really understand this."

She looked me square in the eyes with tears covering her little 12-year-old face and shook her head yes; then she flung her head down and nuzzled into the bunk bed mattress, sobbing. We were both a mess from crying. All I could do was stroke her back for a bit and tell her I loved her. I then kissed her wet cheek and left for the airport, deeply grieved over that goodbye.

This was so difficult and not what I bargained for. I never expected to be torn so incredibly by what God was asking me to do. Through the tears, I felt God speak to my heart once again that Esther represented the many other children who are suffering and have no one fighting for them, whether though the injustice of hunger or untreated sickness or from abuse. If we do not continue to fight, then who will? I had to stay focused.

In Liberia, international adoptions are closed at this point in time, so it isn't even an option right now. Most of the children we work with are unadoptable internationally for numerous reasons. But having children who I love still there truly puts a fire under me to make sure all these little ones and their friends are not suffering. It keeps me very determined to make sure they are all properly taken care of. In circumstances where international adoptions are an option for a child, I fully support them. It is such a wonderful thing. At the same time, we always have to keep in mind that adopting one child out of a needy orphanage into a foreign country is not the answer for all the needy children in that home. We need to stay motivated to go back and help the many others.

For me, it is about falling in love with these kids and choosing not to forget that it is our responsibility to act on behalf of their futures. It is our duty to do what we can to make sure they all grow up emotionally, physically and spiritually healthy, while inspiring and enabling the locals to help their own. If a child is in distress and we can adopt them out of that orphanage to save their life or give them a healthy future, then we work hard with others to get them out. But if the child is not in distress and is being properly taken care of, then an international adoption may not be the best thing for that particular child. They have something to offer their country as they come into adulthood, if they are raised well. We have to have incredible wisdom with this. Each case is so individual.

We believe that raising children in an institutional setting is not a healthy alternative to living with a conventional family in a supportive environment. But sometimes we just have to make those scenarios work with what we have. It is also vitally important to mentor the locals in caring for their own in a healthy and loving manner.

I often refer back to the orphanage home we helped bring into existence in Benin as a wonderful example of children who are being raised with a heart for each of their villages and for their whole nation as well. They hold the keys to bringing change in their country as they grow up with a whole new value system through Christ. If we had started that home with the sole intention of adopting them out of their country, whole villages may never have been given the opportunity to know Christ and learn a new value system for the future generations. I have personally learned huge lessons that not all situations are created equal. God has to guide us in all these endeavors.

I bless all of you who have and will adopt children internationally. My prayer is that you will raise your children with their culture in mind and a heart for their people. As they are raised in a privileged life, may they never forget where they came from, and may they grow up to be the world changers that they have the potential to be because of their upbringing. **Your adopted child has a high calling on their life, and it may very well be to transform their native land for Christ.**

For me personally, my calling is to the thousands of orphans who need us as parents to fight hard for their existence, all along caring for each individual child in front of us. Serving physically as well as helping them understand and experience God's love and compassion for them is our mandate. It is up to us to make sure they do not suffer any longer from empty bellies or nightly rapes from awful caretakers.

Esther knows she is my special girl. She watches me like a hawk in whatever I do. She prays the most amazing prayers of protection and empowerment over me, asking God to equip me to help the many other children in her country. Even though Esther wants to come home to America with me and craves my daily affection as a mother by her side, she also has a glimpse into the magnitude of what she is giving up by allowing me to come and go from her life as I do. Her love is beautiful, her sacrifice is humbling and her depth in God is powerful. Being twelve, she is still a child, but Esther does get it. She wants other suffering children to be helped as she was. She has a glimpse and depth in God that only comes from walking through tough stuff. The orphanage director I leave her with is a phenomenal mother who shares my love for Esther as well as all the others in her care daily. Because of this, I am able to fight for the many others who do not have that.

As Michael lay in the hospital bed in pain and near death, we all questioned if God would heal him from hepatitis, or if this would be the end of Michael's life here on earth. His life was hanging in the balance.

We had met Michael a year prior to his hospital stay through our Child Development Program at one of the children's homes we were helping in Liberia. He was a bright 18-year-old at the time, very eager to learn all that he could about life.

We found out that Michael was never wanted by his family as a child, and he endured incredible neglect growing up. He basically raised himself. As a neighbor put it, no one cared if Michael lived or died.

When we met Michael, he had only been apart of the children's home a short time and was trying to finish school. He was at the top of his class and took his studies very seriously. He was also very eager to learn about God. Through our program, if the kids want a Bible they can earn one by memorizing all the books of the Bible. Michael was the first one in his group to do this. He loved his new Bible and began to study it daily. He was great at always being prepared for his small group each week and eagerly soaked up all that was covered during these sessions.

We learned not long after we met him that he suffered from hepatitis. Our staff immediately took him to the doctor and got him on a treatment plan. Our field nurses, Mariel and Debbie, took personal responsibility for making sure Michael did not miss his treatments each week. They were quite amazing in this process. Our team grew to love

Michael through the year and showed him more love than he had seen in a lifetime.

With incredible grief, our field team learned that Michael had breathed his last breath in May of 2010. This was extremely painful for all of us who loved him. Michael's life was cut way too short. We wanted more on this Earth for this hardworking, smart and kind young man. At the same time, the beautiful and redeeming part of this story is that Michael had an amazing love for God and believed in Him with all his heart. We know he was immediately escorted into Heaven upon breathing his last here on earth. He is truly in paradise now with his Maker. Right before he died, he said he wasn't afraid of death. He said, "If God heals me, I will walk out of this hospital. If He doesn't, then I will have a resting place in Heaven." Through the grief of loss, we are thankful that we had the privilege to be a part of Michael's life. We know we made a difference — an eternal difference.

May we all keep fighting for those who cannot fight for themselves, wherever they may be in the world, and not waste our time on activities that will sap our time, energy and money with no clear objective. Purposeful living for the sake of helping others is key in facilitating the healthy change we want to see in the world.

"Speak up for those who cannot speak for themselves; ensure justice for those being crushed. Yes, speak up for the poor and helpless, and see that they get justice."(Proverbs 31:8-9)

Questions for Personal Reflection:

- Is there injustice happening in your neighborhood?

- Are you willing to be involved with finding a solution?

- Is there an unjust situation abroad that tugs at your heart?

- How can you start small to help in that matter? Give, send, go, be an advocate?

Rebecca and Esther

CHAPTER 13

SERVING WITH EYES WIDE OPEN

"Injustice anywhere is a threat to justice everywhere."

– Martin Luther King Jr.

"Mama, we need food. Please help us; our children are suffering. You cannot turn your back on little children who are hungry. You must bring us some food," said the orphanage director. I replied, "We have helped you for one year, yet you have not followed through with anything we have asked you to do. We cannot continue to help you. It is time for you to call the social welfare office and allow them to find homes for these children. It is very clear that you cannot take care of them. You're not even trying. We have done all we can and we must say goodbye."

What we didn't mention to this orphanage director was that we had uncovered a huge amount of neglect and abuse in the home, and we were now turning the home over to the social welfare office to bring permanent closure. Sexual and physical abuse of little girls were among some of the offenses, and this man needed to be shut down immediately. This had to be done by the social welfare department.

After a year and a half, this man continued to get support from somewhere abroad for reasons unknown to us, and the social welfare office was not able to acquire adequate evidence of neglect. Just recently, we stumbled across the organization who was not only supporting them, but actively moving forward to build them a brand new orphanage and school which would keep them open for years to come. This was a shocking discovery, as we had been working so hard to make sure this man would never be in a caretaker role again. He deserves a prison sentence – not a supported life so that he could continue to abuse those kids.

I made a personal phone call to the leader of the organization. She hadn't had any idea that they had been supporting such a dysfunctional individual. To them, he seemed nice enough, and they just wanted to make sure he had what he needed to help children. They had sold the idea to some wealthy people who were going to fund this large project, and now the organization had a dilemma. Would they do the right thing and pull out their support so the social welfare department could deal with the home, or would they just move forward with the idea to save face with their supporters? This was a tough one for them.

Time and time again, we stumble across Westerners who have an amazing heart to help orphans, yet have no idea that much of the help they come with could bring incredible damage in the whole system of bringing justice to the children. A year ago, I was informed of a mega-church near our hometown that was preparing to go to Liberia on a mission trip to help an orphanage. They were filling up a huge container of supplies and sending over thousands of dollars worth of materials for that home. Excited at the fact the church had a heart to help the children in Liberia, I called the team leader to offer our services on the Liberia side to facilitate their efforts. In finding out the details, my heart sank as I realized the home they were going to help was actually on the government's closure list. I had personally assessed that home a year prior, and I knew for a fact that this was not a home that should remain open.

After sharing very graciously with the team leader the facts of the matter, this person assured me that they were going forward with their efforts and that everything was already in place. They did not need our help or advice in the matter. The woman assured me they knew what they were doing and fully trusted the person who they were working with in Liberia. I emailed one last time with the offer to follow-up in Liberia with the orphanage once the team left the country for accountability reasons, but the response was a short, "No, thank you. We have it covered."

Just recently, to my surprise, I was on the same plane headed home from Liberia with some of the team members who had gone on that very trip last year. They were returning from a different mission trip, helping a school this time. They had no knowledge of my advice to their team leader the year before, but I asked how that mission trip to the orphanage home had gone. These team members did not hold back anything. They gave me a huge earful about what an awful experience it turned out to be.

The home was horrible. The director should never have been responsible for so many kids, and he ended up dying six months later. The team members said that, because of their experience with that home, they would never help an orphanage again in such conditions.

They then proceeded to tell me that they were now helping a school with a great reputation in the country and that they were just going to focus all their efforts and finances there from now on. It was safer that way; they wouldn't be hurt again. I was very aware of the school they were helping and knew of numerous organizations and churches from the West who were also helping them, sending endless support their way because of the great advertising the school does on the internet. They were not lacking in resources by any means.

As the team was talking, my heart was sad. I envisioned the long list of orphanage homes we have built relationships with. They all had amazing and trustworthy directors who desperately needed the help and would utilize every resource to the fullest. Many are real community leaders who help everyone around them, even though they have next to nothing. They are struggling incredibly just to survive but still give of themselves to others. But because most people do not even know they exist, they struggle incredibly. There are many corrupt and negligent directors, but there are also many honest ones. You just have to do your homework to know which is which. We have come across many people who have not taken the time to do this. They are easily sucked into the emotion of it all, and then real damage is done. A great book on the subject is called *When Helping Hurts*. Anyone planning to do work overseas would benefit greatly from reading this book.

To be successful, it is important to educate ourselves and understand who we are working with. It is also extremely important to partner with people and ministries that are already on the ground in these countries doing great things. We have the experience to guide those who want to help make sure every dollar is put in honest hands and every resource given can be used for its intended purpose.

Through our experience, we have found that many orphanage directors fit into one of these categories:

- Directors who are amazing leaders in their communities and will duplicate everything we do for them. They are hard workers and really utilize all the opportunities that we offer to help them become self-sufficient. These are the ones we invest in. We put them on a five-year plan to get their homes up to sanitary conditions, start small businesses and bring the children up to a healthy place through our child development program.

- Co-dependent directors who are not necessarily using the kids as a business but are looking for handouts and a sponsor for their home. They really do not want to put in the effort it takes to become self-sufficient. Frankly, for many directors, it's simply easier to beg than to plant crops, raise animals, run a business, etc. We allocate resources to these directors only so far as to ensure the safety and welfare of the children – that is, medical care, responding to a food shortage, emergency repairs to a roof, etc. We speak into these directors' lives very strongly on a personal level, encouraging them to take responsibility. We are also very open with the social welfare office as to what we see, with hopes they will put legal pressure on these directors to step it up in their care for the kids. One of the greatest challenges with this group of directors is the poverty and post-war mentality, which is characterized by short-term thinking and living in a survival mode rather than planning for the future. We are constantly challenged with how to assist and motivate these directors to make changes that will have a lasting effect and cause a transformation to take place in their lives and homes; the children in their homes will ultimately mimic the behaviors modeled by their "parents".

- Corrupt directors who are using the kids as a business solely for personal gain. Many abuses occur under these circumstances, including the trafficking of children. After finding such an establishment, we cooperate with the local government to help in any way possible to see that the orphanage is closed down and the children are transferred to a safer environment.

We have found the same categories among pastors. Just because they have the title of Pastor or Reverend before their name does not mean you will necessarily find integrity and trustworthiness. We learned this really fast in Liberia and Benin. Unfortunately, many use their title for personal gain. We do know and work with some incredibly honest and trustworthy pastors, but they are sometimes difficult to find in the parts of Africa where we work. We encourage concerned individuals to do their homework and consult with credible ministries on the ground before partnering with just any local pastor.

Working with the honest and God-fearing pastors is incredibly important because they are truly the movers and shakers in their nations. Their hearts are focused on seeing their people transformed through Christ's love and power. They are leading many out of corrupt and selfish lifestyles and are bringing about healthy change on a larger scale – more than we could ever do on our own.

My friend, who is running the orphanage in Benin, is married to one of these amazing national pastors. He is leading the charge for change in every area of injustice. He has founded 15 churches and spends all his waking moments mentoring and raising up other pastors and leaders to follow after Christ's example to be a conduit for change in their country. He is daily challenging people to stand against corruption and injustice.

With each visit back to Benin, I am seeing more and more godly people step into powerful leadership positions. These are the ones who will be ushering in the change this country needs to bring value and worth to each human life. This cannot happen without them. We are seeing this in Liberia as well, which gives us incredible hope for their future, too.

When we link arms with these honest individuals, it makes for a powerful team, able to facilitate God's highest will to be accomplished in these otherwise dark and hopeless places.

The key to success in any country is to always stay teachable. I try to glean as much as I can from others who have been doing this kind of thing for years. I also remain open to what God is saying to me personally – to "think outside of the normal boxes." Experience has also played a big part over the last 13 years – seeing what works and what doesn't as we have tried many different strategies to help the poor and needy around us in a variety of ways.

Wherever we travel, it is always a challenge to have white skin. In many war-torn countries, children are taught from a young age that if they can just get a white friend then their troubles will be over. They believe we have the resources to help them out of all their troubles. We see this predominately where there has been a big influx of humanitarian aid coming into a country. They feel they are entitled to our help. The challenge we face when responding to this mentality is that it removes their personal responsibility to help themselves. Changing this mindset can only be done through building personal relationships and taking the time to be a real friend. Time is always hard to come by, but this is the only way people in these circumstances will succeed and have healthy futures. Coupled with that is relying on wisdom and experience to dictate when we provide a straightforward service in order to meet a pressing, critical need and when the setting is right to empower, coach, train and teach others. Many times kids are caught in the care of negligent leaders, and that is what we are trying to change.

When working in developing countries, this model is one that we are now using with great success:

- **Show all those who cross our path that we find value in who God created them to be, being very careful not to talk to people as if they are less intelligent than we are.**

- **Help people understand that God has not forgotten them; it is so important that we always push people back to relying on God, not us, as their lifeline.**

- **Find out in what areas people are gifted. What kind of skills and talents do they already have? What would they possibly like to learn?**

- **Explain that as God guides us to help financially, we want to see those receiving the resources begin to help themselves. We want to see if they are willing to walk through this time of working hard with the little bit that they are entrusted with. All along, we tell them exactly what our expectations are, even putting these expectations in a contract format for them to sign. Many love the formality of these things.**

- **If we see people working hard and helping themselves, then we entrust a bit more to them. If we do not see them do this, we pull out and work to bring justice to the children in another way through local government intervention.**

All along we work intentionally to restore their dignity if it has been lost. When we do not have the resources to help, we still make the effort to form relationships and pray to show that we love and care for them.

During a recent trip to Africa, one of the head officials in a social welfare office was venting a few frustrations about organizations that were causing some distress for them. This person said to me, "We never have any issues with your organization, and we trust Orphan Relief and Rescue completely in your work with us and with the children, Rebecca." "What makes you trust us so wholeheartedly?" I asked. "What makes us different to you?"

"It is because you are in our offices helping us help the children on a regular basis. We know you do not just care for the vulnerable and orphan children in our country, but you also show how much you care for us personally as social workers. You have shown that you are not here just to do your own thing and show others that you can do it better than us; you do what you can to enable us to do our job well. When you help us write a document, you do not put your name attached to it. When you help us solve issues, you do not care to ask for the credit. We see that you are truly here in our country to help the children and us, and you have no selfish motives behind what you do. You never try to hide anything that you are doing. When an issue needs to be addressed, you include us in the process and allow us to make the final decisions. We know you are working with us, not against us."

The official proceeded to tell me that some organizations come into their country with their own agendas and do not consult or even involve the government in their endeavors at all. They come in and do their own thing, not taking into account what the existing social service agencies are trying to do for their people. "It is counterproductive not to work together," she said with a frustrated look on her face. "They come in, do their thing and then just leave. No one really even knows what they have done, or what messes they are leaving behind. It's just not right. We are here after everyone is gone, and if they do not work alongside us, what they start cannot continue successfully." As I walked away from this woman's office, I was amazed at her bold statements.

After reflecting upon what we as Orphan Relief and Rescue have done successfully, I would have to say that we have always made it a priority to come alongside the social welfare offices in the different countries where we have worked. We know that to affect change throughout the whole country, we have to start with the government. As relationships are built and value is established with those in command, favor is given and a respect is formed that allows us to speak into things that we normally would not be able to speak into.

We have seen incredible results in Liberian and Beninese social welfare offices by working alongside them in a spirit of mutual respect and love to accomplish so much for the children in need. We have learned the importance of not working separately from them but allowing them to have full ownership of what happens to *their* kids in *their* country – empowering *them* to make the difficult decisions. We are seeing justice served for the children and corruption significantly diminished; because of the respect they are given, they do not want to see us disappointed.

Long-term changes in Africa and other developing countries will only last if we value those whose efforts have gone before us. With regard to government officials, corrupt or not: they are in authority, and we have to work with them if we want to see real change.

When we value people, we can truly affect positive change by sharing and encouraging them in healthy and honest ways of living. This can only happen through friendship.

Questions for Personal Reflection:

- Are you a teachable person who is willing to take advice from others, regardless of whether they share your culture?

- Would you be willing to change your plans for the good of those whom you are serving if you realize you are wrong in how you are proceeding even if it causes some humiliation on your part?

- When you see corruption happening in front of you, do you stay away and complain about it, or do you get right in there, valuing those involved, so that you can affect change for the good?

- Are you willing to be a part of the solution and influence positive change around you?

CHAPTER 14

~~~~~~~~~~~~~~~~~~~~~~~~~~~~

REDEMPTION DISCOVERED

~~~~~~~~~~~~~~~~~~~~~~~~~~~~

"We want to avoid suffering, death, sin, and ashes. But we live in a world crushed and broken and torn, a world God Himself visited to redeem. We receive his poured-out life, and being allowed the high privilege of suffering with Him, may we then pour ourselves out for others."

– Elisabeth Elliot

Wade was very thin and weak, and we knew he was not going to live much longer. He was soon going to be another casualty from AIDS. His withered and frail body was difficult to look at now, and our hearts broke for this man. Tim met with Wade once a week, along with the many others at the local AIDS hospice in our hometown in Texas. This was in the late 1990's and early 2000's, when AIDS hospices began to spring up across America due to the large number of HIV/AIDS patients that could no longer live on their own with their illness.

We knew that Wade might only have a few weeks or even days left to live, so Tim put a plan together to give Wade a surprise outing. He knew that Wade loved fishing. Wade often talked about how he always wished his dad had taken him fishing, even just one time. This was one thing that really stuck out in Tim's mind when he heard about Wade's very difficult upbringing.

When the big day arrived for the field trip, Wade had no idea where Tim was taking him. He was in a wheelchair waiting on the front deck when Tim drove up. His withered body was all bundled up in a huge fluffy coat that engulfed him completely. Being a black man, his huge smile with big, white teeth was a priceless sight. He was so excited he could hardly contain himself. He was very weak and had no strength, yet his anticipation of this day had wiped away all emotional signs of distress.

Tim recalls how his heart broke as he physically lifted Wade's body into the car and held this grown man's frail body in his arms. Tim said he remembers thinking about how difficult this process must have been for a man who was once very self-sufficient. Now he was completely dependent on others because of what this disease had stolen from him. Tim said he had to hold back his emotions at this point so as not to let Wade realize how difficult this was for him. Tim did not want to ruin the great adventure he had waiting for Wade.

Tim's surprise was to take Wade fishing at a local lake. Wade was so excited and full of emotion as Tim put him into the boat and rowed out into the lake. Tim said Wade's huge smile was a permanent fixture on his sunken face the entire day, and nothing was more rewarding than that. They did not catch a single fish, but Tim said it was the best day ever for Wade and that words could never be adequate to explain how amazing it was for him to give Wade this gift. It broke something in Tim's heart, as well as in the hearts of all of those who heard about the experience. Wade told Tim this was the best day of his life. He thanked Tim over and over for that gift. Tim still has a hard time talking about that day he spent with Wade without being filled with deep emotion.

Wade died a couple weeks later, and Tim was so thankful that they were able to share this experience together as great friends. Knowing a dream was fulfilled for this man was priceless. At the funeral, Wade's mother and relatives thanked Tim over and over for investing in his life and caring enough to make a dream come true for Wade during his last days on earth. His mother said, "We are forever indebted to you for this." Tim said he knew he was just doing what he felt God wanted him to do.

Tim has been a huge example to me in the area of loving people. I have never met someone who knows how to love people so genuinely and quickly with no strings attached as my husband does. People all around him feel loved and cared for.

Around the age of 30, seven years into our marriage, Tim hit rock bottom in his life personally, making some very poor decisions. After much heartache and difficult choices, he knew he had to make some serious changes in his life or our marriage would not make it and our kids would suffer. Through some very tough years and conscious decisions, Tim recommitted his life to God and worked hard to get to know God in a more purposeful way. This commitment and pursuit of God has forever changed his life, as well as our whole family's life and all those in his path. Tim is a completely different man. He has allowed God to refine him and make him into an amazing husband, father and friend. He is very passionate about helping others understand their purpose in life, and I have seen Tim truly love people to Christ in some pretty amazing ways, through friendship and action as he follows all God prompts him to do.

When we committed to work with the young adult program at Mercy Ships in 1998 until it ended in 2006, Tim wanted to instill in the students a need to give of themselves to the community around them. We can all dream about going to a foreign country to show God's love there, but unless we are doing it in our own neighborhoods, we will never be fully effective abroad. Once we learn it at home, we can be successful wherever God may lead us. And that is where this ministry with the AIDS hospice came in.

Tim took students weekly to this local hospice (as well as to some other service-orientated places nearby) to show them how to love those who have been, in a sense, discarded by society.

I will never forget when Tim went to the hospice for the first time to check it out. He said that it was very difficult for him with his own insecurities about what types of people he may encounter in this particular home. Would they welcome him, or would they really not want any visitors?

When Tim entered the home, he went around and met the different residents, introducing himself to each one. Most of the residents there had been shunned by their families and had no one to take care of them in their dire need for full-time care. They ended up in this home feeling alone and abandoned by those who should have loved them most. The ones living in the home at that time had mainly contracted HIV/AIDS through intravenous drug use or homosexual activity.

The Centers for Disease Control and Prevention estimated in 2011 that as many as 1.2 million U.S. residents are living with HIV infection or AIDS. About a quarter of them do not know they have it. About 75 percent of the 40,000 new infections each year are in men, and about 25 percent in women. Around half of the new infections are in blacks, even though they make up only 12 percent of the US population. In the mid-1990s, AIDS was a leading cause of death. However, new treatments have cut the AIDS death rate significantly. [12]

The first person Tim met at the AIDS hospice was a man named Marion. In his own words, Tim recalls his first encounter with this man:

I looked Marion right in the eyes and extended my hand to shake his. I said, "Hello, my name is Tim. What is yours?" When I shook Marion's hand, he became very emotional and said, "No one has extended a hand like that to me in years. Thank you for not being afraid to touch me. Even the mailmen do not even touch our mailboxes. They leave the mail beside the box." Marion gave me a bit of an overview of what it was like as a man living with AIDS in this part of Texas (this was 13 years ago; lots of progress since then has occurred). All of these things surprised me.

Over the next few years, Tim faithfully went to this hospice weekly. He took the students in each school he led to the home, giving them a chance to become a part of the residents' lives.

During this period of time, each man and woman living in this home was deeply affected by Tim's love for them. Tim never judged them, only loved them. He did a Bible study at the home each week, always directing them back to God's love for them and His desire for a personal relationship with each one. All but one made a personal commitment to God and wrestled through the things they knew they needed to deal with. We had the pleasure of watching some truly broken people learn to have a love relationship with Jesus. They were able to forgive others and themselves through the process. We regretfully had to see many die, but we were so grateful that they found their peace with God and were ready to meet their maker when they did pass away.

On the other hand, we are excited to say that some of them are still alive today. Through the years, antiviral medicine has improved significantly. This has allowed many hospices around the United States to close down because those infected with AIDS are living much longer and healthier lives if they continue taking their medicine. The stigma surrounding the HIV/AIDS virus has also dramatically decreased in the United States.

One man named Harry (whose name has been changed to protect his anonymity) is going on his 28th year living with HIV/AIDS. He is currently in college, studying to become a lawyer. He is no longer in a hospice setting and is living independently. When I last talked with him on the phone, he informed me that he still has five years to go before he gets his degree – but he's going for it nonetheless. He said as long as he stays on his medicine, his white blood count should stay up.

When we first met Harry in the hospice, he was quite a troubled man. He had experienced some very terrible things in his life. As a man living the homosexual lifestyle, he had been disowned by all his family and friends. One day shortly before we met him he and his partner had been at a park in Dallas when a group of young men approached them, violently harassing them for being homosexuals. Before Harry knew what was happening, these young men took out a gun and shot them both, leaving them to die. His partner died in his arms that night. Harry said it was the most horrific experience he had ever encountered. Harry was miraculously saved, yet he wished he had also died that night after losing the only person in his life he felt had ever really loved him.

Through many long conversations and hours of investment into this friendship, he became very close to our family. We all grew to love Harry. Late one night, Harry called Tim, deep in thought and full of questions. After much contemplation, he knew that accepting Jesus as his Lord and Savior was the only way to really experience true freedom from everything he had dealt with in his life. He desperately desired to be free in his spirit. That night on the phone, Harry accepted Christ as Lord and Savior over his life. He became free that night.

Harry likes to write, and at that time he would write out his different thoughts and send them to us in the mail. He regularly wrote thank-you letters as well, letting us know he appreciated the investment we made into his life, loving him unconditionally.

These letters came right before he committed his life to Christ.

Dear Tim,

Before I hit the sack tonight, I just had to get this down to you, because it is that important. I want to give you and all the young adults you bring to the house a big time Thank You!!! Personally, I was reminded that there are good people and good things going on in the world. It is very easy with all that I had to endure for me to have a very negative, cynical outlook on life. There have even been times I have thought of suicide. Your being here and sharing yourselves and time with us helps to restore hope and faith to me that life is worth it, and I can make something worthwhile of it.

-Harry

Tim,

I am writing to say I had a super fantastic time with you and the young people the other night. Seriously, those young people are like another world from what I am used to in my social and past personal life. I can relax and do not have to be on guard because they have the spirit of Christ shining forth from the inside, and there is nothing to fear. My interaction with them is a big eye-opener. It makes me think, "Harry, where have you been all your life?" The realization makes me a little sad too, because I have wasted so much. Yet the experience with them has made me want to change in a major way many things about me. When I see their commitment to Christ and that spirit that is in them, I want it, but feel incapable of having what they have. And I envy them too, for what they have. I just thought I knew what being a Christian was and that I was on par. It is like I met people from another planet and I find them so where I want to be, I want to leave and go there. Not one time have I felt judged – just loved and accepted, and that is so different from my experiences with other Christian groups. This more than anything has caused me to reflect on the way I live, since I came into contact with you people. I love you all beyond words for this priceless thing.

Soon after that came the phone call to Tim that changed Harry's life once and for all. Harry wrote this down afterwards and gave it to us to keep as a reminder of his new commitment.

Salvation has come to me because I gave my everything to our Blessed Savior, Jesus Christ, on the phone in a prayer led by Tim Pratt, late in the night of December 5, 1998. After witnessing Christ in the young people Tim brought to visit us, I could not help but see what I have longed for all my very lonely life. These young volunteers gave me something that very few in my very large family rarely gave me: total, completed, unconditional love and acceptance! When these wonderful people first arrived, briefly I doubted them. Why? Because I have received so much rejection because of my illnesses, and this was far out of the realm of my experience.

The cruelest, most painful aspect of having AIDS is the rejection and shunning of me by my nine brothers and sisters and not being part of their lives or the lives of their children. There has been a deep, black, bottomless, void in my heart on account of this. When I looked in the mirror, I saw nothing looking back and nothing worth loving or caring for. Because of the love of Christ in Tim, I ate at his table; his children played at our feet as I learned from him of my Savior. Now I see a good man looking back at me in the mirror.

-Harry

Learning to be Jesus with skin is the key to watching Jesus come alive in others. God is looking for those who will be His hands and feet to the many who are hurting.

God is Love, and 1 Corinthians 13 spells this out for us very clearly. If we will truly commit to walk out loving others regardless of what they have done in their lives, or what society they have come from, or what lifestyle they live, our whole world will be changed. **Let us be the conduit which God can use to be an outward expression of His real heart to all mankind – whatever walks of life they come from.**

Each year around 2.6 million people worldwide become infected with HIV and 1.8 million die of AIDS. The worst region is sub-Saharan Africa, where in a few countries more than one in five adults is infected with HIV. The epidemic is spreading most rapidly in Eastern Europe and Central Asia, where the number of people living with HIV increased by 54.2% between 2001 and 2009. [13] These numbers are staggering. And each life lost is incredibly valuable and has a story such as our dear friend Wade and the many others who will not be forgotten.

In our work in Africa, we are seeing more and more children orphaned from AIDS. The number of orphans in some sub-Saharan countries exceeds one million and, in some countries, children who have been orphaned by AIDS comprise more than half of all orphans nationally.

AIDS is responsible for leaving vast numbers of children across Africa without one or both parents. In some countries, a larger proportion of orphans have lost their parents to AIDS than to any other cause of death. [14]

The ways in which we are able to help the orphans with AIDS are different in each country. We have seen in the poorest areas the negative stigma of AIDS is a huge problem. If anyone finds out an orphan has AIDS, or that their parents died of AIDS, no one will come near that home. It is a cursed home in the community's mind. So we have to handle each case very delicately.

When I started helping the first orphanage in Benin, I had my suspicions about which children had AIDS. They were the skinny sick ones who would not regain their health no matter what we did for them. Being proactive, with the permission of the orphanage director, I paid a doctor to come and test all 109 children for AIDS, TB, sickle cell anemia and a number of other diseases. I was determined to get all the information needed to appropriately treat every child correctly.

The children's screams could be heard throughout the whole neighborhood as they were pricked for their blood tests. It was a pretty traumatizing day for all of us. My solace came through knowing we were only putting the kids through this trauma so we could help them.

After a week of waiting, I went with the orphanage director to the doctor's office to get the results. She let us know that all the children were HIV/AIDS negative, some with just a few minor sicknesses – nothing major. I was completely floored by her results. I knew this could not be the truth. I called my friend who lives there, and she was not surprised a bit. She said, "Of course you were going to get that response. There is no way the doctor or director would ever tell anyone the real results for fear the community would find out any of the kids had AIDS. This would be social suicide for that home." I was livid, but there was nothing more I could do with that. So this was the beginning of some hard lessons learned while trying to help.

Now my approach is completely different. We educate as a whole and treat every individual case differently according to where they live and who their guardian is. We are working hard to change the stigma associated with AIDS in the countries where we work. It starts with one person at a time.

On one of my visits to an orphanage we are helping, I could not take my eyes off of a little four-year-old named Joseph. He had fallen asleep standing up while he was singing corporately with the other 59 children. He was absolutely adorable. It was suspected that his parents died of AIDS, so he was tested when brought into the home. He tested HIV positive. There is no free antiviral medicine in his country unless the person is on his or her deathbed. So for now, little Joseph was given a homemade drink of ginger and lemon juice each day to keep his stomach from hurting so he could eat normally and stay healthy. You would never have known he was HIV positive. He looked like a normal, healthy boy, and for that we were grateful. As I watched him, I was thanking God under my breath for his life; I was also asking God for wisdom on how to find a means of treating him and the many others in his identical situation.

We cannot avoid the blatant message that Christ modeled when he walked this earth. Leprosy was the AIDS of that time period in human history. What did our Lord do with those whose skin was oozing with leprous wounds, or who had lost limbs to the disease and were living in outcast caves beyond the borders of society? He reached out and looked into the intrinsic value of each individual human soul and extended a hand to them in love and compassion.

The need for us to be involved at one level or another with the AIDS epidemic is huge. The numbers are too appalling to avoid it. Educating ourselves on the problems, needs and stigmas in different areas with regards to the AIDS issue is key in order to learn how to affect change. No two places are alike. It is each of our duties to love these precious children and fight for their lives in whatever capacity we can. If we won't, then who will?

Questions for Personal Reflection:

- Do you have prejudices towards those with HIV/AIDS?

- Do you have prejudices towards those in the homosexual community?

- Will you commit to loving all those in front of you equally, knowing each person just wants to be loved and not judged?

CHAPTER 15

HOPE IN THE EYES
OF THE DESPAIRING

*"Our life is full of brokenness – broken relationships,
broken promises, broken expectations. How can we
live with that brokenness without becoming bitter
and resentful except by returning again and again
to God's faithful presence in our lives."*

– Henri Nouwen

Hooked up to an oxygen machine, Ann looked very frail and sick. When I walked into her room, she tried to say hello but could hardly speak because of how weak she was. I knew she had just come out of the hospital, but the nursing home staff could not tell me why because of medical confidentiality rules. I did not know the severity of her condition until I saw her with my own eyes.

As I bent down to kiss her, she very carefully and slowly, through her paced breathing, began to tell me that she had been in the hospital because of lung cancer complications; she had almost died there. She really thought that her time on earth was up. She said she tried finding my phone number because she was calling all her friends to come to the hospital and say goodbye, but she could not find her address book. She really did not think she was going to last through that week. She had made her peace with God and had prepared herself to die. The whole process was very scary, yet she knew where she was going, so she knew she would be okay. The hospital had drained over a quart of fluid from her lungs, and now they would just have to see if her body could hold on a bit longer after this procedure. There were no guarantees though. The hospital released her back to the nursing home to either recover or to die.

I didn't want to stay long, because I knew it was really difficult for her even to talk, and she needed her rest. I thought this was my goodbye to Ann, that this may be the last time I would see her on this side of Heaven. As I prepared to leave, I bent down and kissed her on the forehead, then told her that I was going to pray for her before I left. I told her that with all the miracles God has done in her life, surely if He wanted to, He could heal her completely again. That would be my prayer for her. I laid my hand over her chest and pleaded with God to bring healing to this precious woman. I asked God to do another miracle as He had done so many other times in Ann's past.

After my prayer ended, to my surprise, Ann took my hand and began to pray a very precious prayer over me. Through each word, she would gasp for air as she struggled to keep up her breathing. Oh, was my heart breaking! Tears welled up in my eyes as I thought of this woman in so much pain, trying to be a blessing to me. I was deeply moved by her gesture of selflessness. Her life truly humbled me. Walking out of Ann's room that day, I knew the hand of God had touched me through Ann's life.

I first met Ann when I was volunteering at her nursing home about a year prior to this incident. For years I had been passing this nursing home four times a day while taking my kids to and from school. I knew my church was volunteering one Saturday a month at this particular home, and I loved knowing they were doing this because there is a huge need to encourage these ones that are often forgotten by society. In my mind, my days were already occupied with my travels to Africa, orphanage work and volunteering for children's church one Sunday a month. My plate was full; there was no time to do even one more thing.

As I was driving by the nursing home one day, I felt like God prompted my heart just to go in and meet the residents. I shrugged it off and made a comment in my heart to God that I didn't have time for that. Yet that nudging did not go away. Each time I passed, for about three months, I would feel that same nudge. I was finally a little perturbed with God, and I reminded Him of all the things I was already doing for Him. God began to deal with my heart about what I was spending my time on. I really felt Him tug my heart to begin making my days really count – every hour, not just in the overall sense. Evening TV was something that I was using as a brain-dead time, but that needed to go. No more "Survivor", "Amazing Race" or other shows that were really taking a block of my time.

I finally got out my calendar and said, "Okay, God. My calendar is full, but I feel I can commit to every Thursday from 1:30 -3:00. But that is it." I sensed God speak to my heart. "I will take it." I then let God know that I was already emotionally spent with my current duties and that this was just me saying I would go to build friendships with these people, with no agenda. I really did not have anything to give except maybe a listening ear. But I would go.

The very next Thursday, I walked in looking for any staff that could help me. They all pointed me to the activities director. I explained to her that I would like to come in to volunteer for a short time each week, and I asked if she would be okay with me just hanging out with the residents – talking and playing games, getting to know them and building friendships. She looked at me and asked if I knew anyone or had relatives there. I said, "No, I do not know anyone. I will need someone to introduce me to them." She gave me a puzzled look and said, "Lady, you must have a whole lot of time on your hands." "Well actually – no," I replied, "but I pass by here every day, and I just know this is what I am supposed to be doing." She still looked confused but said she would love for me to come each week, as they never have enough people to interact with the residents.

She took me from room to room until I had met all 42 residents. For the months to follow, I listened to countless stories of lives lived to the fullest. Some residents would tell me very disheartening life stories, while others told me great, inspirational stories of lives lived well. Playing dominos also became of great friendship-builder. Little did I ever envision that this would become one of my favorite times of the week.

As much as I have loved on these residents, I have felt even more loved by them. When I come into their rooms or the dining hall during a meal, they light up like a Christmas tree. They instantly want hugs and kisses. I am told how beautiful I am, how sweet I am, how I am like the daughter they never had, how cute I look that day. They have doted on me beyond words.

As I got to know the residents, God started to prompt me in different ways to encourage and challenge them to greatness, even within the confines of their nursing home. To my complete surprise, God started to do some really crazy miracles through these relationships. I am brought to tears as I recount these amazing God stories.

It all began with just being a listener – valuing them for who they are, and how they lived their lives, encouraging them to continue to live to the fullest and not give up. "Until you are in the grave," I would tell them, "you are still alive, and God has intended each of us to live an amazing and fulfilling life with Him until we are ready to meet Him in Heaven."

When I first met Ann, she was a very depressed woman. Already having been in the home for five years at the age of 79, she had no hope for a future because of her health issues. She felt completely stuck. She was bored and could not see what anyone did in a nursing home except learn to pass the time until death.

Through many conversations with her, I found out that Ann had fostered 16 kids in her young and healthy years. She was an amazingly strong woman who took care of everybody around her. She was always given the most difficult kids by the social welfare office because they knew she could handle it. The kids were always ones that no one else would take due to their drug addictions and very troubled pasts. As I would listen to these stories, I was amazed by how strong she had to be in God to walk through these tough things that she chose to do to help others.

After a couple of months, I felt like I was to begin challenging Ann in her own life. "Okay, Ann. I have heard all these stories about your life. You were one strong lady with God. You did all that you did by staying really close to God – and now what are you doing? You are just sitting here depressed. Ann, are you ready to have these last years of your life be the most amazing ones? Do you want to see God do amazing things through you?" She looked at me and said, "Of course I do. I just do not see how that could be possible." I then asked her these questions. "Ann, what makes you come alive? What is something that you like to do that makes you really feel God's presence in your life?" She got a big smile on her face and said, "It's playing my guitar. I totally come alive, and I really feel God all over me when I play." I asked her where her guitar was. "It is under my bed," she replied. "Well then, I think it is time to get that guitar out and start playing it," I told her. "I have a problem," she said. "I can't play it in my wheelchair because of the wheelchair arms." I told her to try to figure out how to get a wheelchair without arms; I was sure that someone there would help her do this. She agreed to pursue this idea.

The next week when I checked on Ann, I could tell instantly her countenance was different. She looked at me and said, "Guess what? I am playing my guitar, and I got a wheelchair with arms that can go up or down so I can play as much as I want!" "Wow!" I replied. "How has that been?" "I love it!" she said. "I have felt so close to God. This has been a great week." I told her how proud I was of her for working hard to get the right wheelchair so she could play again. I was so happy to see her regained excitement for life that week.

Then the time came for me to give my next challenge. "Okay, Ann. It is wonderful that you are so happy this week and that you feel so close to God. Now how about you consider giving some of your joy for others to experience too? Would you consider going to different rooms where you know people are really hurting or depressed and maybe playing guitar to encourage them like David did for Saul in the Bible? I can guarantee that you will feel even more of God when you begin to minister to others." She looked at me reluctantly. She said, "There's only one problem with that scenario." "What's that?" I asked her. "Well, I like TV too much. I don't have time to go visit different rooms because all my shows are on, and I don't want to miss any of them." "Okay, Ann," I said. "I understand, but what if you were to think of one hour in the day when the shows are not that great, and take that one hour to go room to room ministering to those residents in desperate need of encouragement?" She thought for a moment and then responded. "Well, I guess from three to four p.m. there are not many great shows on TV, so I could probably do it then." So that day in her room, she committed to me to go room to room from 3:00 to 4:00 each day that week to minister to others with her guitar.

To my surprise, the next week she was beaming again. She was smiling from ear to ear when she saw me. "Oh, this was such a great week!" she exclaimed. "I ministered to people in their rooms, and I have been ministering to people in the dining hall. And oh, I feel God all over me." All I could do was smile and get teary eyed as she was talking, telling me about her ministry times. "Ann, you got it, lady! You really got it," I told her. "Oh, I have it alright," she said. "And when I brushed past one man in the dining hall, he stopped me and said that he felt something really peaceful come over him when I touched him. All I could say was that it was God — because God is all over me and all through me!"

After her testimony, we had a little prayer time in her room, thanking God for this renewed love and passion for Him. We also committed to the future whatever He wanted to do through her life there. Now let me tell you – Ann can pray. She then started to minister to me by speaking encouraging words over my life. The workers and nurses kept peeking into the room because it definitely got a little loud. I know God was smiling down on us that day in Ann's room. And I still smile when I think of where Ann had come from: depression to life.

After my visit with Ann when her lungs were pumped of fluid, I had to travel to Africa for two weeks. I really did not believe I would see her again after that goodbye. To my shock and excitement, when I returned and went into her room, she was sitting up and looked wonderful. "Oh, my goodness," I said, "you look great! What in the world happened? How can you be doing so well after such a trauma only two weeks ago? I thought it was the end." Ann had a big smile on her face and said, "Well apparently God is not done with me yet! After they took all that fluid out of my lungs, they took numerous x-rays, and they cannot find the cancer in there anymore! No one can explain it." "Ann," I said softly. "Are you saying that you are healed, that the cancer is gone?" "Yes, I guess that would be the only explanation. I guess I can say that God has healed me." She said this so nonchalantly, as I just sat listening in shock. Not that I don't believe in miracles; I was just so amazed at God. She recently let me know that a tiny spot is still left on her lung which was missed in the original x-rays, but the doctors assure her this will not be what ends her life. Her lungs are doing miraculously well.

Over two years have passed, and Ann has continued to be a huge encouragement to the staff and residents. She is full of faith, hope and love for others. God has restored her passion to help those around her as she has pursued renewing her walk with God.

Another woman deeply affected by God's redeeming love is Beth (changed name). She is a 49-year-old woman who has a nerve disease which confined her to bed for over a year. She was told she had no hope for recovery and given a terminal diagnosis with this type of nerve disease. Whenever I came to say hello, she was always pleasant and smiling, yet I could sense her deep despair under the circumstances.

After a few months of just saying hello weekly, God woke me up one night and strongly impressed on my heart that I was to pray for healing over Beth. I did not know her well, but I committed to God that when I was there on the following Thursday, I would pray for her healing.

When I went to Beth's room that next visit, she seemed extremely depressed. I asked her what was wrong. She told me that the state had just dropped the insurance which enabled her to continue her physical therapy. They felt it was a waste of their money and time, and with her diagnosis she was only going to get worse, not better. Physical therapy wasn't helping her in their opinion. She was very discouraged over the news she had received that day. My heart sank for her, but then I regained my faith, knowing what God wanted to do for her. I then proceeded to tell her that God had woke me up in the night and that I felt I was to pray for her complete healing. She told me she did believe in God and healing and that she knew God could heal her if He chose to.

Even through this I knew she was going to need extra encouragement along with prayer. I bought her a CD player and worship CDs to begin renewing her mind and spirit. I also encouraged her to be reading her Bible, as she was in a very despairing place. Each week I could see her countenance changing, and there seemed to be hope in her eyes. Week by week she began to regain more mobility. Beth is no longer confined to her bed 24 hours a day. She is very mobile now.

A few weeks ago, I was talking with someone in the dining hall, and I spotted someone running down the hall towards us in a walker. As she approached me, I said, "Oh my goodness! Is that Beth?" As she saw my mouth drop open, she said, "Oh yes it is! I can run now. Every chance I get, I am running with my walker down here." Tears filled my eyes, as God once again amazed me.

It has been very interesting how each person at the home has brought on a completely different challenge. One of the more difficult challenges came in the form of a gentleman named Buddy.

My first encounter with Buddy was over a game of dominoes. He knew I did not play well, and he definitely wanted me to know what a horrible player I was. After a very insulting game I just wanted to get as far away from this man as possible. After the game he lingered at the table a bit and kept on with his rough and tough attitude. He asked me who I came to see at the nursing home. I told him I come just to visit, and that I have lots of friends there. He let me know how insulted he was that I had never visited him and that I must be biased towards certain ones in the home. "Well, I only come to see the residents who want me to visit them and are nice to me," I said. To my surprise he then asked if I would begin to visit him. I told him if he would be nice to me I would agree to visit him. So then and there he agreed he would treat me kindly.

Buddy was a very angry man. He was not happy he had to be stuck in this nursing home due to his health, and he hated that he had lost full control of his life. He had only recently come to live there when his wife was no longer able to manage all his health issues on her own. In his younger years he was a very well-known referee for many college baseball teams and some basketball teams. He was always in high demand. He also ran a whole department over the road construction projects going on in Dallas, Texas for years. He was even an elder at a church he had attended for over 30 years. In these positions, he was boss, and he was proud to say he was the best at what he did.

Now he was stuck in this nursing home. He was miserable and really didn't care who he hurt around him. The staff did not know what to do with him, and the residents stayed away from him. It was a real problem. My challenge to Buddy was to make these years be the most amazing and rewarding years of his life: speaking life and not death, leaving a legacy, being someone who others felt loved by, being someone who was a giver not a taker, forgiving others and not holding grudges, practicing all that he preached in his years in the church, having God go from his head to his heart.

It is wonderful to say that Buddy has made a huge turnaround in his life. He is no longer an angry man. I had a staff member pull me aside recently and tell me that Buddy is treating her like a princess now. She said she couldn't believe it. "I just want to say thank you for being his friend and for coming each week. We can tell it makes a huge difference in Buddy's life, as well as the many others. And it makes our job easier."

Buddy and I have a very unique friendship. He knows he is loved unconditionally, but I am also pretty hard on him if I hear he is treating people badly. He's all rough and tough and full of smoke, but I see that God has truly gotten a hold of his heart.

God has completely knocked down my stereotypical view of nursing homes due to this newfound love for these precious people who are obligated to be in those homes with their ailing bodies. This nursing home experience has become an amazing highlight in my life; I've seen God do some crazy things. I think He is finding it humorous to show me some pretty radical things up until the very last seconds of these people's lives.

In a place known for death, I am seeing life. In a place where there is so much hopelessness, I am seeing hope. In a place where people have been discarded by society, similarly to the orphans in Africa we work with, I am seeing amazing value and worth. In a place where there is no hope, I am seeing people look to the future. Where people should be waiting to die, I am seeing excitement for life.

Questions for Personal Reflection:

- Are you a blessing to the elderly or disabled people in your life?

- How can you bless someone in your life this week who is an outcast, hard to reach or considered undesirable?

- Will you be willing to pray for the people in your path who are sick?

~~~~~~~~~~~~~~~~~~~~~~~~

CHAPTER 16

LIVING FULLY ALIVE

~~~~~~~~~~~~~~~~~~~~~~~~

"The ultimate measure of a man is not where he stands in moments of comfort and convenience, but where he stands at times of challenge and controversy."

– Martin Luther King Jr.

Tears streamed down Andrew's face as he explained to my husband that he had been sent to our summer program by his father and had no intention of listening to anything our speaker had to say that evening or any other evening. He was just there to pass the time until he could go home.

What he did not expect, however, was to be so deeply affected by what our speaker, Rob Morris, had to say that night about God's passionate love for him. God reached very deep into his soul, and he could not deny God's heart and love for him any longer. He had never experienced such strong conviction in all his life. Drugs, girls and gangs were just a few of his confessions. The most difficult thing for him was trying to figure out how to actually accept God's forgiveness for all the terrible things he had done. Being only 16, and a pastor's son, he knew he had been running from God for years. This was not going to be easy.

My husband Tim embraced Andrew and told him very directly that God forgave him and wanted him to walk in complete freedom and restoration. He was living with so many secrets and lies. The bondage and despair that tormented him daily were unbelievable. He said his family had no idea of what he had been involved with. He had become a master at lying. Through hours of tears, prayers and confessions, Andrew began a whole new journey that night in pursuit of a relationship with this passionate God.

During this time, my husband was the director of young adult and youth training programs at the Mercy Ships International headquarters in Texas. Side by side for six years, we had hundreds of young people come through these programs until 2004. Watching my husband in action with these young people has definitely been a highlight for me over the years. Tim has an amazing gift with this age group. He has literally affected positive change in thousands of lives over the years due to his love and care as a father and mentor to so many, always directing them to Christ. Many of the young people who came through our programs were fatherless. Their fathers had been absent for one reason or another, and the deficit they would come with was enormous. We could always spot the ones who had grown up without father figures. Some of them did have fathers or stepfathers that lived in the home, but they had zero connection and very minimal interaction with them, leaving them just as desperate as the ones with absent fathers.

After Andrew made all his confessions and recommitted his life to God, Tim told him that if he really wanted complete freedom and accountability in his life, he would need to tell his father everything he had been a part of. He also needed to confess all the lies that he had been telling his family for years. This was critical for him in order to avoid going backwards when he went home.

Andrew looked at Tim in shock and voiced an absolute, "No way. I could never do that. This would crush my family. I just can't. Please do not make me do that, Tim." Again Tim shared that if he was really serious about making a complete turnaround in his life, this had to be done. Through deep soul-searching, Andrew agreed he would do this as soon as he arrived back home.

Five days into that program, we loaded up a bus with teenagers and our own three kids and headed on our 18-hour journey to Monterrey, Mexico. Once in Mexico we had many activities arranged for these young people to expose them to helping people who were in great need and sharing testimonies of how God had made a difference in their lives.

Andrew definitely brought a lot of life to the group. In just five days we could see his whole countenance had changed. He was free, and he wanted everyone to know how great he felt. While on the different bus rides to ministry locations, Andrew was the one speaking boldly to his teammates about getting rid of all the junk in their lives and living for all that God had for them. He was also the one guiding everyone in prayer for the local people we were there to serve. He was quite a passionate speaker. Each time we listened to him, my husband and I would look at each other and smile, remembering where this boy had come from. This was great to see, but at the same time I was also breathing prayers to God for this young man. I prayed that all his words would really come into practice when he arrived back home.

A few days into the Mexico outreach, he was given the opportunity to share his testimony with a large crowd who had gathered around our team. He shared with incredible passion about how God pursues us and desires to have an intimate relationship with us. He also shared that in the last eight days, he had felt more freedom inside than ever before in his life. "This is real life," he declared. After he shared, a local pastor came up and shared how people could receive Christ into their hearts and feel this freedom Andrew was talking about.

When asked if anyone would like prayer, a young man from a local gang came forward; he was deeply convicted by Andrew's testimony and moved to surrender his life to Christ. The pastor later shared with us that this gang member made radical changes in his life and has been growing in his faith in Jesus ever since. He also became an active member of the church, allowing this pastor to really mentor him. The pastor said this young man would come early each Sunday to set up chairs and often brought his former gang members to services. Some of them also came to know Christ through watching the transformation that had taken place in their friend's life.

Little did Andrew know the impact his life would have in the suburban town of Monterrey, Mexico, all thanks to his choice to surrender his life to God. Through his freedom, he was able to see others set free in Christ. Witnessing this transformation in his life and the lives of those around him was truly incredible.

Andrew's father was not an absent father; he was just a busy man in ministry who felt his son was simply going through teenage stuff that he would grow out of. He and his wife prayed for their children, but they admit they had no idea how much trouble their son was in. Once his son's confessions came, knowledge of all this would completely change the course of the whole family's life.

We got a very surprising phone call from Andrew's father a few weeks after he arrived home. His father thanked Tim for the investment that he had made in his son's life. He was also so grateful that Tim advised Andrew to confess everything. He said he could not believe how radically transformed his son had become.

He shared that Andrew had affected their whole youth group as well as their entire church body. He was also eager to see how Andrew would do going back to school. He was convinced his son was going to affect his whole school for Christ, too. He said, "Everyone wants what he has, this freedom. What Andrew brought home is a passion for God that we all want." The father later flew Tim and me up to their hometown in Tennessee to speak at a youth retreat and at a meeting for those parents who wanted their kids to come to our program the following year. They were not going to let their kids miss out.

That following year, Andrew returned with his sister, as well as members of their youth group. They all made strong commitments to God for their future that summer. **Andrew's commitment to God had a spiral effect on numerous lives, helping put them on the path to true freedom.**

Andrew has stayed strong and passionate for God through the years. He recently experienced some near-death health trials but continues to walk closely with God. Throughout all the struggles of life, we are so proud of this young man for choosing God's highest even when life does not go the way he feels it should. He continues to be a great example to all those in his path.

Matthew's life is another redemption story. Drinking night after night in order to numb the tremendous pain of betrayal, rejection and loss was not what this young man had planned for his life. Just two months before his wedding, he found out his fiancée was cheating on him. Matthew had asked the woman of his dreams to be his wife, and now his plans for a future with her were completely shattered. To add to this heartache, a day after he would have been married, his closest friend Thom died in a drowning accident. The loss was unbearable, and he did not know how to deal with such deep despair.

How could he live a normal life again? In just two short months, his whole world had been shattered. How could he ever allow himself to love so deeply again? How could God take his best friend at the young age of twenty-two? Thom had his whole life ahead of him. Matthew was devastated, and all he could do was drown out his sorrows with the bottle. The alcohol was his cocoon of self-protection to try to deal with his emotions. For the next ten months, his life was little more than a blur. He simply existed with no purpose but to stay numb, just so he could make it through another day.

Matthew says the hardest part was losing his best friend. Thom had just graduated from college with a teaching degree. He believed that one man truly could change the world, and Matthew wholeheartedly agreed. The two would talk and dream for hours about how they were going to make a difference with their lives. That was the number one reason Thom got his teaching degree. He wanted to make a difference in this world.

Ten months after Thom's death, Matthew realized his friend's pursuit of helping others became all he could think about. He realized he was not living out his beliefs, and it was time to put what he believed into action. Thom had pursued his dreams, and now Matthew felt he had to take on the challenge in memory of Thom, who was never going to be able to fulfill what he set out to do.

Matthew mustered up the courage to make some real changes in his life. He decided he would take a year off and join Mercy Ships to help others. Sailing on one of their ships and working in the galley was what this gentleman signed up for, and this is when our worlds came together.

Our introduction to Matthew sparked immediate friendship. He stood out to us as a kind and gentle young man who seemed to hide behind a big head of hair and an overgrown beard. We were immediately drawn to his heart for those around him, and we could see that he was eager to serve those in need. With that in mind, my husband (who loves to give people a real African experience), asked Matthew to come on one of his up-country village excursions. He was going to deliver some food and other miscellaneous supplies to a group of people who were just returning home to their village after being displaced during the civil war in Liberia. This was the same food we got in South Africa that you read about earlier. After four hours of crazy, rugged driving, they arrived in this remote village. As the villagers were guiding them around, Tim saw that Matthew was an immediate child magnet. The children were drawn to him and followed him everywhere. He was clearly uncomfortable with children, and it was evident he did not quite know what to do with all these kids. Tim let him know that all he really needed to do was just sit and allow the kids to touch his white skin and play with his hair and beard. They were intrigued by this burly white guy and just wanted to check him out a bit. My husband said he enjoyed watching Matthew's world being shaken up a bit through these kids. Little did Matthew know this would be the start of what God would use to soften his heart for what was to come.

Later on, when Tim and I started helping an orphanage that hardly had any food, Matthew quickly jumped in and started helping too. He made it his mission to buy rice and other food items each Saturday to get the children through the week without going hungry. I later asked Matthew about this experience and this is what he shared with me regarding that time.

After being on the ship for six months, I felt content. I was doing what I was supposed to do, and I was feeling more at ease. This was exactly what I needed. Then I saw the kids suffering at the orphanage, and it was such an emergency. **It was my dare-to-be-great circumstance. It was not humane to do nothing.** *They were living in demoralizing, sick and subhuman conditions. It was a shock to see children living this way.*

Tim and I, along with Matt Le Page and other ship volunteers, took on this home as a side project. This was Fatu's home, which you read about in Chapter 5. I could see week by week Matthew's heart was beginning to soften with the children at Fatu's. He loved on them, and they loved on him each Saturday he was out there. I could see a different person emerging from this young man. A new kind of passion started forming in Matthew to help others in his path. At that time he also spearheaded another fundraising effort to facilitate building a home for a needy family. This was George's home, which you previously read about.

By the end of our six weeks helping Fatu's orphanage home, it was time to leave Liberia. Goodbyes were now in order. Matthew and I, along with another young woman, went to the orphanage home one last time to say our farewells. This was not an easy thing.

As children started to cry, I decided I would make a quick break and just give a general and quick farewell. I gave a couple of them hugs then waved a big goodbye as I climbed into our taxi. I did not want to lose complete control of my emotions at that point. This was already too difficult. I was thankful that my exit went fairly smoothly. I then watched the others as I sat in the taxi. The young woman was crying as she hugged a special little boy whom she felt extra bonded to. Then she made a quick break towards the taxi, waving goodbye to them all with tears dripping down her face. Then we watched Matthew. This was when the magnitude of what had been happening during these last six weeks in his heart became very evident.

Matthew went from child to child (all 80 of them) and hugged each one of them individually with a great bear hug. And he cried and cried. This was not a short ordeal; this was a drawn out and painful goodbye. The children were a mess, and he was a mess. I could not believe what I was witnessing. I was watching this man completely break. It was something I had never seen before.

When he finally got in the taxi, he was a totally devastated and continued to sob as we drove away. We would later learn that the neighbors came over at different points in the day to see if someone had died because they had heard so much crying from the children throughout the day.

As Matthew was grieving in the taxi, I told him, "Oh Matthew. You are so not done with Liberia or these kids; this is only the beginning." He did not respond to me at that time. He was too much of a mess, but I know he knew it deep in his heart too.

After we all returned to America, we asked him to come work with us when we started Orphan Relief and Rescue. He was one of the first four staff members who accepted the challenge of setting up the office and programs in Liberia.

Matthew has been through a lot of things in these last few years, and he has had to choose to give God all of his hurt and pain. Looking at him today, it is hard to believe all the hard stuff this man has walked through. He is a reminder to me of God's amazing love and heart to bring each of us into complete freedom if we will choose to walk closely with Him. It is also a reminder of God's highest for each of us – to live fully alive, free of the bondage this world would entangle us with. To our excitement, Matthew has since married an amazing Liberian beauty and in June 2011 they had their first child. The redemption story continues to unfold as we work alongside this completely changed life, a man who has chosen to use his life to bless others, daring to live for greatness.

Questions for Personal Reflection:

- Are you willing to be a mentor figure to a hurting young adult in your path?

- What are some things you can do to help someone who is emotionally hurting?

- Is there a "dare-to-be-great circumstance" that you are feeling prompted to act upon?

CHAPTER 17

REWARDS OF A
MERCIFUL LIFE

*"In ordinary life we hardly realize that we receive
a great deal more than we give, and that it is only
with gratitude that life becomes rich."*

– Dietrich Bonhoeffer

*"It's not what you believe that counts; it's what you
believe enough to do."*

– Gary Gulbrans

In January of 2002 I got the call from my sister in
Washington that my mother had passed away suddenly.
All I knew at that point was that she died of complications
from diabetes and congestive heart failure.

A few hours after the call, confused and shocked, I
boarded a plane headed for Seattle in a complete mess of
tears. I was glad I was sitting next to a window so I could just
look outside and not have to explain my tears to anyone. I
had no idea how to process the death of someone so dear
to me. "How do I deal with this God? I don't know how
to process these emotions." I looked out over the clouds

as we ascended into the sky, and I felt like God spoke to my heart these words. "Be thankful. Thank me for her life. Thank me for the years you had with her. Thank me for what she added to your life. Thank me for everything she represented." So with tears dripping down my face, for the next four hours of flight overlooking the fluffy white clouds, I did just that. It was incredibly difficult, yet precious at the same time. By the time I reached Washington, I could begin the mourning process of walking through the goodbyes alongside the rest of my family.

Many of us have seen a loved one die, which has made us keenly aware of our own mortality and the realization that our lives here on earth are very short. Material things will come and go, but our souls will last forever through all of eternity. We will either spend our time in Heaven with our maker, or we will spend it separate from God. All that we do here on earth will determine how we will spend our eternal lives. Bruce Wilkinson's book *A Life God Rewards* explains this so well. He uses the illustration that our lives here on earth are like a dot, and all of eternity is like a line that extends from that dot:

He talks about how most of us spend so much time and energy planning for our retirement, yet we rarely take into account our real future. The future that matters the most for all of eternity is not going to be spent here on earth.

After my mother died, my sisters and I had to go through all her stuff and decide what to do with a lot of the things she held dear to her heart. We realized very quickly that a lot of things that my mother cherished did not carry the same value for us. Many of her treasured material things, such as the 60 pairs of shoes under her bed, meant little to us. It all made me really sad. All the energy and time she had put into different things didn't matter at all in the life to come.

Yes, of course we kept some sentimental things that we will cherish because Mom loved them – but even then, these too are temporary, and none of us can take any of this stuff with us when we die. The thing my mother did leave with us that we will take into all of eternity is her love for God, for us and for all those in her path. She was a real lover of people and was generous to those around her.

There is a story that Jesus told in the book of Luke about Lazarus and the rich man. This story really drives this point home. Jesus wanted us all to deeply understand this concept.

Now there was a certain rich man, and he habitually dressed in purple and fine linen, gaily living in splendor every day.

And a certain poor man named Lazarus was laid at his gate, covered with sores, and longing to be fed with the crumbs which were falling from the rich man's table; besides, even the dogs were coming and licking his sores.

Now it came about that the poor man died, and he was carried away by the angels to Abraham's bosom, and the rich man also died and was buried.

And in Hades he lifted up his eyes, being in torment, and saw Abraham far away, and Lazarus in his bosom.

And he cried out and said, "Father Abraham, have mercy on me, and send Lazarus that he may dip the tip of his finger in water and cool off my tongue; for I am in agony in this flame." But Abraham said, "Child, remember that during your life you received your good things, and likewise Lazarus bad things; but now he is being comforted here, and you are in agony. And besides all this, between us and you there is a great chasm fixed, in order that those who wish to come over from here to you may not be able, and that none may cross over from there to us."

And he said, "Then I beg you, Father, that you send him to my father's house – for I have five brothers – that he may warn them, lest they also come to this place of torment." But Abraham said, "They have Moses and the Prophets. Let them hear them." But he said, "No, Father Abraham, but if someone goes to them from the dead, they will repent!"

But he said to him, "If they do not listen to Moses and the Prophets, neither will they be persuaded if someone rises from the dead. (Luke 16:19-31, NASV)

When we read the story of the rich man and Lazarus, it is apparent that what we do with the resources available to us on this earth will directly impact our eternity. The rich man can be any one of us who have access to resources in the bank or within our own network of friends. The poor man, Lazarus, could represent those who are hurting here in America, or those in a foreign country who are suffering from starvation and disease.

What we do with the resources that pass through our fingers will impact our eternity. Jesus said "In as much as you do it for the least of these you have done it unto me." Are we following the way of our culture and living a self-absorbed lifestyle? Or are we choosing a lifestyle of sacrifice in order to bless others? I believe God is calling us to diligence on whatever platform He has given us to serve from. He is calling us to build His kingdom, not our own.

True spirituality is doing everything we do with all of our hearts unto the Lord. If the Lord is calling you to make money, then work hard and use that money to help others and bring people into the knowledge of who God is. If He is calling you to serve somewhere, then serve with all your might. Whatever He is prompting your heart to do, do it with all you've got for His glory! Choosing to sacrifice for the sake of all that God asks of you puts you in alignment with the purposes of God and impacts your spiritual and practical life.

I recently turned 40, and I have to say this year has been a year of reflection for me. I believe the key to happiness and wholeness in life is to walk closely with God and to be someone who gives to others. I want to use my life to help bring solutions to the problems in this world. I do not want to be someone who adds to the problems. I am dreaming like I will live forever, yet I am living like I may die today. One of my favorite quotes, written anonymously, is: *Until you are prepared to die, you are really never ready to live.* I can honestly say that I am living in such a way that if God decided to take me home to Heaven today, I would be prepared in my spirit to go. No, I do not want to die today. I want to be here for my kids and husband. Yet I am learning to keep short accounts with others, as well as to deal with my internal "junk" daily. I am choosing to surrender my emotions to God. Living in this manner frees me up to not live in fear of the future.

With each new thing that God asks of me, I still question and ponder in my heart. But my trust in Him has grown so much through these last years. I do not hesitate as much anymore before I go forward. Each day I live in awe of how rewarding and fulfilling it has all become. I am experiencing the most amazing journey by using my life to help others.

This does not mean our lives are easy by any means. On the contrary! Life is very difficult and full of trials. We encounter so many crazy things that happen due to the work we are involved in. Through all the trials and hardships, God is always there and always giving us what we need, when we need it, to get through each of these hard times. That is His commitment to us as we walk forward.

Isaiah 58:10 talks about God taking care of us as we take care of the needy: *And if you give yourself to the hungry, and satisfy the desire of the afflicted, then your light will rise in the darkness and your gloom will become like midday. And the Lord will continually guide you and satisfy your desires in scorched places, and give strength to your bones, and you will be like a watered garden, and like a spring of water, whose waters do not fail.* I have seen this verse come to life. God does guide us, He does satisfy and He does give strength to our bones. We do feel like a watered garden wherever we go. We are satisfied.

A businessman recently asked me a question as I became teary-eyed sharing stories about the kids we are helping. He asked, "How can someone like you who is so practical and matter-of-fact be on the other hand so mystical and emotional when it comes to what you do in Africa?"

I responded by saying that as I see the suffering children and their caretakers, I cannot help but feel God's heart breaking for them and be tenderized by God through my involvement in their lives. It is very humbling to be part of miracles and answered prayers for these kids. We are regularly making life and death decisions for the children and constantly need God to guide us in all of this. God has touched me in ways that I could not have imagined possible. I feel His presence in my life so strongly as I do the work and share the stories. It is often difficult for me to even put these experiences into words.

As I was recently reading a devotional by Oswald Chambers, he so adequately described what I was trying to put into words with this:

Has Jesus ever looked at you? The look of Jesus transforms and transfixes. Where you are "soft" with God is where the Lord has looked at you. If you are hard and vindictive, insistent on your own ways, certain that others are in the wrong than you are, it is an indication that there are whole traits of your nature that have never been transformed by His gaze.

So I can say – this is what is happening to me. Jesus' gaze is transforming me as I reach out to the suffering and abandoned little ones. I feel like I have gotten a glimpse of Jesus through them.

Practically, people often ask my husband and me how we can continue to do this work with so little assurance of provision for our future. There are so many sacrifices to make, both personally and financially. We have given up the best working years of our lives with minimal pay to do what we do. **We have come to the conclusion that the only things that really matter in this life are things that have eternal value.** God's word and His most prized creation – people – are eternal.

It has now been almost five years since we started Orphan Relief and Rescue. It is humbling to know that because so many others are also choosing to say "yes", hundreds of children are no longer suffering and have a chance for a bright future. I am so thankful for a very supportive and proactive husband who is equally passionate about making sure the kids get the help they need to survive and thrive. This is very much a team effort. We are equally grateful for great staff and for so many who give toward these efforts. None of this would be possible without these willing hearts.

Our field team continues to amaze me with what they accomplish with such a small budget. They have shown true ingenuity in utilizing every dollar for its fullest impact on these children's lives. My head is always full thinking of the magnitude of what we are involved in. It is an overwhelming task with so many needs around us. We truly have to have wisdom as to what we touch and what we don't. This is definitely a challenge.

With God's help, we will expand into many other needy countries in the years to come. We want to help as many children as we possibly can.

We are taking one day at a time, and we are determined to walk closely and humbly before God and man. We are just ordinary people willing to step out to make a difference in the lives of those who are hurting to change the world around us.

What about you? Are you living the life you know God intended you to live? Many aspects of your destiny have not been determined yet.

There are some things that have been set into motion based on the decisions you have already made in your life, but there are many things that have not been determined yet and will unfold based on the choices you make.

In 1 Samuel 15, I am reminded of King Saul's life in the Bible. He was picked by God to be a strong king who was anointed, blessed and given favor in every area of his life. God let Saul know that as long as he chose to follow Him, God's hand would be with him and He would bless his kingdom. King Saul started off strong following God's every command, but through the years he fell into pleasing man instead of God. Because of this, Saul was not able to walk in all that God had destined him for. He lost the blessing and favor of God and also lost his kingdom. In the 34th verse it actually says God regretted that He had made Saul king over Israel. God did His part, but Saul did not.

Another man that God chose was Jeroboam. He was someone who got God's attention because of his leadership potential, and God anointed him to be king over the Israelites after King Solomon's reign. He was given incredible favor and power. God's destiny for Jeroboam was for him to lead the Israelites in the ways of God. He wanted to give him a dynasty equal to what He gave King David. In 1 Kings 11:38 God said these words to Jeroboam. *"If you do whatever I command you and walk in my ways and do what is right in my eyes by keeping my statutes and commands, as David my servant did, I will be with you. I will build you a dynasty as enduring as the one I built for David and will give Israel to you.*"

Soon after becoming king, Jeroboam also began to please man over God. Leading his people to worship carved idols. These actions caused him never to walk in what God had destined for his life.

Then there are the famous stories we are all familiar with of men and women who did walk in the destiny God had planned for them. They did what God asked and were able to change the course of thousands of lives. Noah obeyed God and built an ark, saving humankind and all animal species. Moses rescued thousands of Israelites from slavery. Esther saved the entire Jewish population from annihilation.

God loves us enough to give us free will. That is a beautiful thing. God will never force our hand in anything. It is strictly up to us how far we want to go in partnership with God.

Can He trust you to do what He asks of you? Are you living in a way that allows God to bless you?

He has big plans for you. His ways are so much higher than our ways. Ephesians 3:20-21 says: *Now to him who is able to do immeasurably more than all we ask or imagine, according to his power that is at work within us, to him be glory in the church and in Christ Jesus throughout all generations, for ever and ever!*

You were meant to live an extraordinary life. Everything you do matters to God and each person who comes into your life. God wants a personal relationship with you. He wants you to feel his heart break for those around you who are in need. He will guide you to live beyond yourself to become someone's miracle in partnership with Him.

Are you ready to come on this journey to change the world around you? Are you ready to walk in the destiny God has for you? It all starts with God then flows out to others.

There are so many opportunities to help others. There are opportunities awaiting you in your neighborhood, as well as across the oceans. There are no shortages of opportunities for you to reach beyond the borders of your own existence. It just takes a willing heart to move forward.

The rewards are endless and so worth the effort. I promise that you will never be the same. Your adventure is waiting.

Live in such a way that God's love can bless you as you wait for the eternal life that our Lord Jesus Christ in his mercy is going to give you. - Jude 1:21 (New Living Translation)

Conclusive Thoughts

The big question is **"Does God really need us to accomplish His perfect will here on Earth?"** Hopefully through reading the stories in this book you have come to the conclusion that God does desire us to partner with Him. He has chosen to work through our hands and feet to carry out His plan here on earth. Yes, He is almighty and powerful and can definitely do the work Himself, yet from the creation of the earth in Genesis 1:28, He handed the responsibility of governance over all living things to mankind.

God did not give up ownership of the earth, but He did give the responsibility of taking care of it to humanity. We are His representatives here. He needs human involvement to bring His perfect will to pass on earth.

Every act of kindness for someone who God prompts us to help opens the door for His highest to come to pass.

All through the Bible, He has chosen to use mankind to accomplish His will, as in the examples given in this book of Noah, Esther, Moses and Daniel.

The list goes on and on of cases where God has shown us how He chooses to use human involvement to bring His plans into existence, and each man and woman had to say "yes" for that to happen.

Every day we are faced with promptings, nudgings and impressions. It is because God wants to do something through us and needs someone's hands and feet to do it.

Second Chronicles 16:9 (KJV) says that the eyes of the Lord run to and fro throughout the whole earth to show Himself strong on behalf of those whose heart is perfect towards Him.

Will you be that one? Can He show Himself to be strong through your life and actions?

As we use our lives for God's purposes, we see amazing miracles happen before us – sometimes big, sometimes small.

Miracles can happen instantly, but in my experience those are rare. I believe the process of acquiring that miracle is just as important as the miracle itself.

God is after our hearts and the hearts of those around us. It is always about Him, drawing all of humanity to Himself. So let's not give up in the process.

What is He prompting you to do today?

As God asks in Matthew 6:10, let's pray, "Thy kingdom come thy will be done on earth, as it is in heaven". Then listen for what God may ask us to do to bring His will into existence. Sometimes prayer is all that God asks, but in my experience there are usually action points that follow those prayers to see the miracles come to pass.

This is where the wild ride begins.

ORPHAN RELIEF AND RESCUE

Orphan Relief and Rescue works with orphaned, abandoned and abused children in Liberia and Benin, West Africa who no one else will help – who have simply been forgotten. We are a grassroots organization helping to bring justice to children in a variety of ways. We are delivering much-needed aid, construction improvements, training and child-development services, to enable children in difficult circumstances to grow up in a healthy manner.

Our focus is two-fold – help the honest, caring orphanage directors who genuinely love children, and work with local governments to see that corrupt and abusive directors are removed from their positions. All the while we strive to make sure kids are rescued from abuse, neglect, and trafficking through a variety of channels.

Our desire is to redeem a lost generation of children. We have studied the problems and tested the solutions – now please consider helping us go the second mile for them. Here are some ways you can take action and partner with us today.

You can visit www.orphanreliefandrescue.org or email info@orronline.org
Opportunities to partner with Orphan Relief and Rescue for Individuals/Groups/Churches

- Sponsor a project or an individual child

- Host a benefit dinner or fundraiser at your church

- Come visit the children in Liberia or Benin

- Be an advocate and pray for the children

- Become a monthly donor, allowing us to have the funding foundation we need to continue meeting these pressing needs

In the last four years we undertook projects at more than 20 orphanages in Liberia and Benin, including...

- 8 major construction projects, including dormitories and school buildings

- 10 wells dug or rehabilitated

- 6 new latrine and shower blocks

- Over a ton of food delivered every month – more than 100,000 pounds to date

- Hundreds of children protected by mosquito nets and screens

- Hundreds of children off the floor and into beds

- Seeds, tools and training to plant hundreds of acres of crops

- Monitoring to prevent abuse and advocacy to protect kids

- Hundreds of children treated regularly for various ailments

- Establishing partnerships with local clinics to provide ongoing primary healthcare

- Breeding animal pairs purchased and distributed for raising

- Child-development team prepares children for healthy future.

To have Rebecca or Tim speak to your group, you can contact them through info@orronline.org

To follow Rebecca personally through her website go to www.rebeccampratt.com

Other Information

For more information about Jesus:

- www.Y-Jesus.com, specifically the article "Is Jesus Relevant Today?"

- www.godresources.org

For more information about Mercy Ships:
www.mercyships.org

BENIN COUNTRY INFORMATION

Government
Type: Republic under multiparty democratic rule
Independence: 1 August 1960 (from France)
People
Nationality: Beninese
Population: 9.05 million [15]
Ethnic groups: 42 ethnic groups, most prominently Fon, Adja, Yoruba and Bariba
Religions
50% Indigenous beliefs (animist), 30% Christian, 20% Muslim
Languages
French (official); Fon and Yoruba in the south; Nagot, Bariba and Dendi in the north
Literacy
39 % of total population
Background:
This West African nation is on the Gulf of Guinea, with Togo on the west and Nigeria on the east. It is about the size of Tennessee. It is bordered by Burkina Faso and Niger on the north. The land consists of a narrow coastal strip that rises to a swampy, forested plateau and then to highlands in the north. A hot and humid climate blankets the entire country.

While Benin has seen economic growth over the past few years and is one of Africa's largest cotton producers, it ranks among the world's poorest countries. The economy relies heavily on trade with its eastern neighbor, Nigeria.

The Abomey kingdom of the Dahomey, or Fon, peoples was established in 1625. A rich cultural life flourished. One of the smallest and most densely populated regions in Africa, Dahomey was annexed by the French in 1893 and incorporated into French West Africa in 1904. It became an autonomous republic within the French Community in 1958, and on August 1, 1960, Dahomey was granted its independence within the Community.

Between 1974 and 1989 Dahomey embraced socialism, and changed its name to the People's Republic of Benin. The name *Benin* commemorates an African kingdom that flourished from the 15th to the 17th century in what is now southwest Nigeria. In 1990, Benin abandoned Marxist ideology, began moving toward multiparty democracy, and changed its name again, to the Republic of Benin. [16]

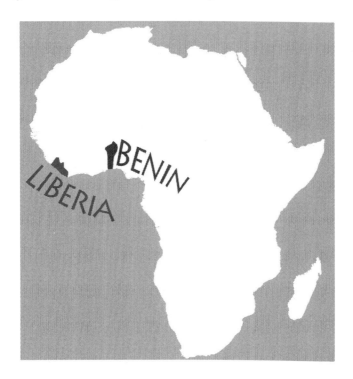

LIBERIACOUNTRYINFORMATION

Government
Type: Republic
Independence: July 26, 1847 (from American Colonization Society)
Geography
Location: Western Africa, bordering the North Atlantic Ocean, between Cote d'Ivoire and Sierra Leone
People
Nationality: Liberian
Population: 3 million
Ethnic groups: 20% Kpelle, 16% Bassa, 8% Gio, 7% Kru, 49% spread over 12 other ethnic groups
Religions
40 % Christian, 40 % Animist, 20% Muslim
Languages
English (official), 16 indigenous languages
Literacy
20-40% (estimate)
Background
Liberia was once a sought after tourist area. It is known for its beautiful beaches and friendly people.

Although founded by freed American and Caribbean slaves, Liberia is mostly made up of indigenous Africans, with the slaves' descendants comprising 5% of the population.

The West African nation was relatively calm until 1980 when President William Tolbert was overthrown by Sergeant Samuel Doe after food price riots. The coup marked the end of dominance by the minority Americo-Liberians but heralded a period of instability. By the late 1980s, arbitrary rule and economic collapse culminated in civil war when Charles Taylor's National Patriotic Front of Liberia (NPFL) militia overran much of the countryside, entering the capital in 1990. Mr. Doe was executed.

Fighting intensified as the rebels splintered and battled each other, the Liberian army and West African peacekeepers. In 1995 a peace agreement was signed, leading to the election of Mr. Taylor as president. The respite was brief, with anti-government fighting breaking out in the north in 1999. Mr. Taylor accused Guinea of supporting the rebellion. Meanwhile Ghana, Nigeria and others accused Mr. Taylor of backing rebels in Sierra Leone.

Matters came to a head in 2003 when Mr. Taylor – hemmed in by rebels and under international pressure to quit – stepped down and went into exile in Nigeria. A transitional government steered the country towards elections in 2005 when Ellen Johnson Sirleaf became the first woman president in Africa. She has ushered the country into peace and development with her leadership.

Around 250,000 people were killed in Liberia's civil war and many thousands more fled the fighting. The conflict left the country in economic ruin and overrun with weapons. The country was left without electricity and running water. Corruption is rife and unemployment and illiteracy are endemic.

The UN maintains some 15,000 soldiers in Liberia. It is one of the organization's most expensive peacekeeping operations.[17]

(ENDNOTES)

[1] USAID 2006 Trafficking in Persons Report and Response http://pdf.usaid.gov/pdf_docs/PDACH052.pdf

[2] USAID 2006 Trafficking in Persons Report and Response http://pdf.usaid.gov/pdf_docs/PDACH052.pdf

[3] World Health Organization Statistics, Updated 2010 http://www.who.int/countries/ben/en/

[4] U.S. Dept. of State-Trafficking in Persons Report 2009 http://www.state.gov/g/tip/ris/tiprpt/2009/123135.htm

[5] U.S. Dept. of State-Trafficking in Persons Report 2009 http://www.state.gov/g/tip/ris/tiprpt/2009/123135.htm

[6] http://www.unicef.org/infobycountry/benin_1511.html

[7] Intercessory Prayer by Dutch Sheets published by Regal Books 1996 Pg. 31

[8] http://www.nlm.nih.gov/medlineplus/ency/article/001373.htm Early symptoms of dengue hemorrhagic fever are similar to those of dengue fever, but after several days the patient becomes irritable, restless, and sweaty. These symptoms are followed by a shock -like state. Shock may cause death. If the patient survives, recovery begins after a one-day crisis period.

[9] http://allafrica.com/stories/201005180952.html

[10] http://www.independent.co.uk/news/world/africa/daily-battle-to-keep-children-alive-in-liberias-orphanages-768343.html

[11] http://rebecca.cfr.org/publication/7753/liberia.html

[12] http://www.aids.org/topics/aids-factsheets/aids-background-information/what-is-aids/

[13] http://www.avert.org/aids-hiv.htm

[14] http://www.avert.org/aids-orphans.htm

[15] http://www.state.gov/r/pa/ei/bgn/6761.htm

[16] http://www.nationsonline.org/oneworld/benin.htm

[17] http://www.nationsonline.org/oneworld/liberia.htm

Made in the USA
Lexington, KY
09 May 2012